THE FALL OF CHRISTIANITY

THE FALL OF CHRISTIANITY
ONLY HOLINESS SHALL SEE GOD

DARRYL MARKOWITZ

FaithWalker Publishing

The Fall of Christianity

Copyright © 2024 by Darryl Markowitz

All rights reserved. No part of this book may be reproduced or transmitted in any form or by any means, electronic or mechanical, including photocopying, recording or storing information in a retrieval system, without prior written permission from the publisher.

Published by:

 Faithwalker Publishing
An imprint of Darryl Markowitz

Cover and Interior Design: Creative Publishing Book Design

ISBN Paperback: 978-1-7374936-8-6
ISBN eBook: 978-1-7374936-9-3

Printed in the United States of America

This book is dedicated to Peter and Rachel
Without whom this manuscript would have
Still been sitting in a dark corner.
Witnesses that the Holy Ghost is real
And does everything that Jesus said it would do

ECCLESIASTES
OR
THE PREACHER

9 The thing that hath been, it is that which shall be;
And that which is done is that which shall be done:
And there is no new thing under the sun.
10 Is there anything whereof it may be said, See, this
Is new? It hath been already of old time, which was before us.
11 There is no remembrance of former things; neither
Shall there be any remembrance of things that are to come
With those that shall come after. (chapter 1 KJV)*

15 That which hath been is now; and that which is to be
Hath already been; and God requireth that which is past.
(chapter 2)

---

*All Scripture within this book are taken from Original King James Version

TABLE OF CONTENTS

Introduction		1
Background		9
CHAPTER 1	Why Christians Believe They're Saved	23
CHAPTER 2	Which Religion? Silver and Gold Have I None	45
CHAPTER 3	Faith, Grace, Works, and Religious Confusion	57
CHAPTER 4	Fruits of the Holy Ghost	93
CHAPTER 5	Even Paul Said You Cannot Be Holy and Sin	113
CHAPTER 6	(Perversion) How Saith Jesus Christ and the Holy Ghost?	157
Conclusion		181

INTRODUCTION

What nation, kingdom, country, or people wants to hear that they have an end, a future point in time where after that point they exist no longer? To any of those, before the end comes, it seems improbable and scoffable. Then, when the end comes, the scattered and torn remnants of them, along with others that dwell near them, look in astonishment at the devastation and destruction. Some weep, and say, This was one of the most beautiful countries (or cities or peoples) and now we are no more. How could this happen? Why?

The world has recently witnessed this many times over, from the conquest of the Americas to the rise and fall of Nazism. Poland, the whole country, fell almost overnight. Closer to the present, we see the fall of Communism and the savagery in former Yugoslavia. Right now, Ukraine is being destroyed, and on the religious fronts, current Pope Francis is destroying Catholicism, with the Methodists in death throes, both due to a different kind of invasion. Yet, even though these occurrences witness to everyone's consciences, people still will make their boasts about their *own* people, country, nation, or religion. If someone were to warn them of impending military, economic, or social, or spiritual disaster, most would scoff and feel within themselves as follows: Destruction only happens to *them*, not to *us*. They didn't do it right. That's why they had disaster. Besides, it all leads to improvements in the long run. Tell that to the folks from the Dark Ages where they lost practically everything from medicinal knowledge to plumbing technology, while spiritual knowledge was closely disseminated by just a few, when in Jesus' time it was freely given to all.

If people scoff at warning signs of failure originating from material, mundane things of the world, then how much more will they scoff at warnings of a spiritual nature? Yet, Christianity, Judaism, and Islam all have in common one belief whose implications forewarn of huge disasters. It is the belief in a single, omniscient, omnipresent, omnipotent, and totally Just God. Though this God is loving, yet, because He is Just, He eventually brings about just punishments on the people who forsake Him, whether it be an individual, a city, a country, or the whole world. Even Jesus Christ, in the Book of Revelation, is foretold to tread the winepress of the wrath of God, and, it is Jesus Christ who opens the seals for the final plagues that come upon the world. And you thought He was just about love?

Specifically, Christianity bases itself upon Jesus Christ but of what does Jesus warn? He warned of Israel's destruction along with many of the glorious things that God added to them. However, they did not believe the warnings until destruction found them and then it was too late, and it had already previously happened to them at the Babylonian Conquest and *many* other times. Now, if *those* people, whom God prepared for thousands of years to be His people, didn't believe God's warnings, it is a small wonder then, that the world of Christianity will not believe when the Holy Spirit of God says that their end is near because they have provoked God, even the Lord

INTRODUCTION

Jesus Christ, to anger. Yet, if a sensible person considered that every week in many of their houses of worship, the religious recount the warnings of the prophets and of Christ concerning the wrath of God, that person would feel that Christians would believe such warnings. However, this weekly affair with the Holy Scriptures is nothing new. The Pharisees, who sought to destroy Jesus Christ, also conducted such weekly affairs.

Who am I to be writing such biting words? I, myself, am nothing without the presence of our Lord Jesus Christ's Holy Ghost inside me, now thirty-one years. I haven't trained in any religious school to study the Holy Bible. I haven't been certified by any, so called, great men. I'm just a person who seeks God with all his heart, soul, mind, and strength and rejoices to do whatever the Spirit of the Living God has for me to do. To my readers, I say, don't worry about who or *what* I am, just judge the words that are supplied here for you and thank Jesus Christ. Don't thank me. I am not worthy to be thanked for anything. Please don't be angry with me either.

Blindness. Deafness. Ignorance and hard-heartedness. The self-will of the religious in the time of Jesus Christ prevented them from hearing and changing for the better. Yet, even though Jesus Christ knew that they would not hear Him, because He loved them, He warned them anyway. Even though Jesus Christ knew that the truth would provoke them to anger, even to the point of availing His destruction, He wept for them. And at the time He was crucified, because the Jews had handed Him to the Gentiles for the Gentiles to crucify Him, Jesus said to them *all*, Father, forgive them, for they know not what they do. Yet, the religious did not even regard that testimony and they hardened their hearts even more, until the destruction that Jesus had warned them about came upon them.

Small wonder then, that many Christians, when they read this book, will not pay heed to its warnings. However, because I love you by the love of God, by Jesus Christ, the Spirit of Understanding from Christ has guided me to write.

Warnings are not without explanation or else why should they be believed? I am going to present the reasons why Jesus Christ is angry with Christianity. It has to do with their chosen ignorance, confusion, and corruption of salvation, belief, faith, grace, works, and sin. Their doctrine is riddled with hypocrisy and the fabrication necessary to cover their inherent doctrinal contradictions. And please do not think it will happen to *them,* not *you.* I have tested *many* Christians of all walks and they *all* possess the same poison, no matter their denomination. Put the actual truth close enough to touch their hearts, and they *all* will call me a heretic, a devil etc. But it gives me no joy to *know* of their impending doom, that I am right and they are wrong, well, the Holy Ghost in me is right and the unholy are wrong. But as God has said, I have no pleasure in the destruction of the wicked, in the death of him that dieth, so also do holy people worry over you! And think, if I did enjoy to see your destruction as your many enemies salivate over in their imaginations that are soon to come to pass, I wouldn't labor to write all this for you to save you before it's too late.

Understand, I believe every word of God and Christ that is written in the Holy Scriptures. But the Scriptures are not religious Scriptures. They are Holy Scriptures. Man's religion is not the same as God's Word or His Way. Just as God did not tell the Jews to be Jewish, but to be holy, Jesus Christ never told a living soul to be Christian or to be religious, but, Jesus also told all to be holy and *perfect* if they wanted to inherit the Kingdom of God. The Pharisees had plenty

∾ INTRODUCTION ∾

of religion and tradition, man's *interpretation* of the Holy Scriptures along with many embellishments.

Some religious might say, But that's *how* you become holy, by being religious. That is a *prescriptive Old Testament* style of worship and sanctification, engaging in *external* means of sanctification via commands, disciplines, and *external* study of the *printed* word of God. That is *not* what Jesus Christ died for! His death, resurrection, and pouring out of the Holy Ghost changed all those processes because the Holy Ghost is *in-dwelling,* teaching and leading us into all Truth from the inside out, as Jesus said, I in thee, and ye in Me, as I am in my Father, and He in Me. That's a pretty strong comparison, isn't it? You get that picture? *That's* not religion. *That's* not belief. It's continuous *knowing* from the inside out.

Why is there no faith that God will send His Spirit of Understanding to a soul who seeks understanding? Why must man always try to master by his own self, the things of God? Yet, that is what religion is based upon, upon self and robbery by stealing what belongs to God and dominating it with one's own self-purpose and desires. Shame, shame, shame on them. God is patient, but even His patience has an end.

To find God, one does not have to belong to any group, religion, or otherwise. Just go home and pray and seek God with all your heart, soul, mind, and strength. Pray and seek within, while you are working, and while you are traveling, and do this in secret for no one to see. It is God's glory you seek and not man's. Be patient until your change comes. But what change am I speaking about? It is the change which all religions do not want people to know because then the people would not follow man. They would follow only Jesus Christ. *That* is why the Christians keep telling you not to forsake the fellowship! So they can make sure they reinforce the poison, the lies that hold *them* captive! You are better off home alone where the Holy Spirit can come to you if you truly seek Him.

I am going to *prove,* by reason, understanding, and the Holy Scriptures that Christianity does not agree with the words of Jesus Christ. In my first book, What is in a Word, which shall be republished sometime in the future, I have done so already! Yet, the feeling of something unfinished rested upon me. The reason for this feeling is that I used the gospels, the direct printed words of Jesus Christ, to make the necessary points. However, the Christian community bases much, if not most, of their thoughts on the writings of Saint Paul and others after Christ. Christians feel *their* words are more relevant, today, than are Christ's words.

So, I prayed to God about that, saying that I know there could not be any contradiction in the Holy Scriptures from Genesis to Revelation, and that I know God doesn't change. The same holy message that is in Genesis must be in John, and the same that Jesus is recorded saying in the Gospel of John must be in Paul. So, I prayed for understanding and I shall present to my readers what has been revealed to me concerning the Word of God following the Gospels. It *is* the same.

I shall quote many Holy Scriptures at length, sometimes large sections, or near whole chapters. These will back up other verses of more brevity. The long quotes are necessary to gain the full understanding of God's message and to prevent the shiftiness present in religion. That is why the religious love to quote only a verse here and another there and be sure to have the interpretation of another man right beside it. In this fashion the religious shift the purpose of the *printed* Word of God into fulfilling their own pockets, I mean purpose,

INTRODUCTION

but . . . they do get paid for all that, trying to be like....errrr.... like a college professor. Aren't all their sermons kinda like that? A lecture, complete with a bit of entertainment to lighten everything up? This book is not anything like that, nor is it written for monetary reward.

Really, length would not be necessary if the religious were open to understanding. I could explain the necessaries in a few paragraphs. I have spoken to many Christians with such brevity and it is their inevitable deafness, stubbornness, and twisting of the Holy Scriptures which has required the length of this book. After one reads this, there will be no place left to twist or turn. Then, one can only accept or deny the truth.

Perhaps, to some, my words seem a tinge on the boasting side. Some felt that way about Paul. Yet, I'd rather boast a bit for truth's sake than be complacent in a lie that will condemn me to eternal suffering. I only hope my readers will take up the challenge now presented to them and test out the claims I have made.

The pure Grace of Jesus Christ be with you and guide you.

BACKGROUND

I begin this book because the understanding afforded to me requires me to write. It is the understanding of life which cries out for others to also understand and take solace in its reward. The rewards of the understanding of life are peace, love, joy, and the discovery of what is truth. Truth being more than just *telling* the truth. Truth is integrity, as be true to *what* Goodness really is, that being God. However, the consequences of understanding are gnawing sorrows to the depths of one's soul, because in understanding a bit of the depths of God's beautiful life brings unquenchable desires to promote the same to other souls. Herein is the consequence of sorrow, because understanding reveals the bitter penalties awaiting those who are ignorant, misguided, and hard-hearted.

The spirit of life within the stoney-hearted is not regarded by them, even though their existence depends solely on it. They do not regard life because they do not understand. They do not understand because they do not consider. They do not consider because truth and understanding of life is nothing to them to be considered.

To the religious, introspection, where *their* spirit of life may be felt and seen, is difficult because their poor minds have been regimented into putting *everything* into a Scriptural box dictated by man's interpretations and limited to their mental capacities within that box, which mostly consists of mere quotes. But to perceive and love God with all your *heart,* you need to also emotionally think and appreciate, especially because love and life are mostly perceived in and by the *heart.* They take for granted the difference between the mind and the heart, between a living human being and a corpse, which if you are only a mind, you really *are* close to being a corpse. Some even believe they get conscious life from dead, unconscious, inanimate chemicals in the *brain,* although they can't explain how, only theorize, and don't realize the difference between the mind and brain either. It's sad because God is Love and Life which they claim to love with their *mind.* Sorry, it doesn't work that way.

Hmm, haven't you been taught somewhere that you *can't* perceive the actual presence of God? That you *can't* understand it? Does *that* make sense when God *is* Understanding and Wisdom and says He delights for us to *know* Him? What Satan has done to you is simply tell you that you *can't,* and because you cannot receive what you *don't* believe, you actually make it so that Satan has told you the truth! He *loves* that, in a sort of devilish way. What is *worse,* is the fact that *all* human beings are made of particular portions of the seven Holy Spirits of God so that all human beings have life, love, truth, peace, understanding, wisdom, and justice in them but in unique proportions for each individual, however, if you cannot perceive God's Seven, you probably can't perceive them well at all in yourself! No wonder you don't trust your heart! You have no clue what's there.

When a human being falls into such a state of darkness, he also takes for granted the difference between one who truly loves God and one who does not. One who loves God is one who loves that which makes him a human being, the pure immutable quintessence of Life, Love, Peace, Truth, Understanding, Wisdom, and Justice. Some of these are appreciated mostly through the mind but others mostly through the heart, but God is all seven of these Holy Spirits in One, and we are supposed to love them *all* with our heart. That's not done by simply memorizing and repeating Scripture.

You're supposed to take the little conscious goodness you are made from and through your *clear* awareness of these seven, you love the Conscious Goodness from whence your little goodness came. Done like *this*, you can actually *understand* what you are loving as little love meets greater Love, little life meets Greater Life! Just look deeply at *what* your little love is and watch it connect to God! Surely this is Understanding, Life, and Truth. However, one who has no real depth of love for God has only the feelings of self, feelings like the dead, dried leaves blown off a tree that flounder in the wind until they crumble and rot. Ahh, such are the thoughts of the mind as they come and go unless brought into the captivity of Christ's Spirit. Feelings in the heart, though, are *states* of consciousness! Oh, right, you *misunderstand* the Scripture which you *think* tells you not to trust your heart. Hmm, then how can you *love* God with all your heart? *Fools!*

Not only all that! The religious are *sure* that they love many people and with God's love beyond this world. Well, true love seeks the *best* that you can be and do for what you love. Anything *less* than that and you had better find a different word for what you are calling love. Unfortunately, the *best* you can be and do is prevented by the poison in Christianity which keeps you with one foot toward holy ground but the other toward the corrupted world. If you *really* want to be and do your best toward God and man then finish this book!

～ THE FALL OF CHRISTIANITY ～

Life is a spirit. Love is spiritual. Understanding is the Spirit that promotes life and love. But all seven inherently promote each other so that there are no borders between them. God has all of these which are One Spirit together. When one meditates upon any of these, he also embraces the others! However, because man only considers his five senses, he is unable to participate well in life, love, or understanding, because they are beyond those meager senses. But people surely try to *master* them, ahh, by memorizing Scriptures. That is a *mental* exercise, but what are you doing with your *heart*?

Here I just described the root of man's problem. He tries to be a master over that which cannot be mastered. The Spirit of God, nor anything which belongs to God, cannot be mastered. How can the Almighty quintessence of ultimate conscious Power, guided by His own perfect, pure, immutable standard of Love, be mastered by anything that He created, when all power of Life is in God's hand?

No, man cannot be a master, but if he wants to partake of Being, then man must eat and drink, meaning that man must sustain on the *spiritual* nourishment of God's Spirit. Eating and drinking is not mastering, but savoring and admitting within one that which saves his life. However, because man cannot control love, life, or even understanding, he takes no part with them. Man's downfall is that he tries to be a master, and with only five senses to feed his small mind, then his creations and forms of thought are riddled with failure, hypocrisy, and contradiction.

Today, man is even so foolish that he thinks he has power to feed himself, even with the bread of the world. Yet, when God sends a famine, man has no power to overrule it. Sometimes man sends food to the hungry but it cannot reach them. A fool might try to fault God for the suffering of man, however, God's vision extends unto the vast future of eternal life. The works that he does are for that purpose, to bring as many souls into everlasting joy and life as possible. If man wasn't so wicked, hard-hearted, stubborn, and contrary to God's purpose then God would not walk contrary to man in the permitting of famines, pestilences, and destructions which try man's soul.

Yet, you fault God and not yourselves when God merely rewards you with a *bit* of the destruction you have inside you, but He allows it to manifest *outside* you in a form you cannot control! What? You do not know you have pestilence, famine, and destruction inside you? No. You don't! However, man's vision is so nearsighted that all he sees is his immediate or near self-gratification. Yet, this is man's choice and he shall be held accountable by the judge of Heaven and Earth.

When one appreciates that God's life brought him to be, and, that, this life which is most essential to the human being is that which man had no say over, then one understands that man's sole purpose and wisdom must be to embrace and glorify this spirit of life (but not to try and master it). Is it not wisdom to glorify that which is most important? Indeed, God is the Life of the life, and, therefore, He is most important.

Yet, for many people, they esteem no purpose to the life they use and because of their lack of appreciation and their chosen ignorance, they cannot fulfill God's purpose for making them. God lovingly lets them use the best that He has, and, instead, man chooses to glorify the things that have no inherent life: self, evil, and the dust of the Earth as if it had its own power to create. God is angry at man for loving, worshipping, and choosing the things that have no life to give them, and, which will cause them to die.

Man's wisdom and purpose is to seek, love, and glorify the Living God. Why glorify anything else? Yet, man has many so called great men that he glorifies. Malcom X, Martin Luther King Junior, Muhammad, George Washington, Stalin, Barack Obama—the list is endless. Is any one of these half as great as Moses was, who spoke to God face to face? Yet, Moses never held himself to be great in his own eyes. How could he, when he was dwarfed by the knowledge and presence of Almighty God, his Creator? Neither did Moses allow anyone to glorify him. Finally, is anyone of those a tenth as great as Jesus Christ? Which one in deed or word could be placed in greatness beside Jesus Christ whom God gave commandment that Jesus should lay his life down and pick it up again, because that through perfect living on Earth, death could be conquered. And, then, through accepting this tried and tested death conquering Holy Spirit of Jesus Christ, man could be saved from sinning and death. Muhammad can't do *that*. A lot more about *that* in my book, *God's Creative Writing*.

Human beings are made with the capacity to understand and glorify life. This soul and sixth sense is what makes us different from the animals. But to the contrary side of the human, they also have the capacity to reject understanding life and to promote everything that is antagonistic to the ways of life, such as hating goodness, envy, greed, fear, and evil for the sake of evil. This also makes us different from the animals. Human beings are able to act strictly for the sake of glorifying goodness or for promoting evil for evil's sake which brings them no gain, such as purposefully causing one to suffer just to watch him suffer. They pride themselves on being higher than animals but they become lower, and saying these human beasts are animals is an insult to the animal kingdom.

God is angry. He has done everything possible for man, pleading with him to live. That is all the God of Love wants. He wants us to live so that He can eternally share his goodness with man. Please understand what the anger of God is. It is because He loves man and wants to do good to man and so God told man how to live. However, man rejects God's way of life to his own hurt and destruction. The more God pleads with man, the harder man's heart becomes and there is no other way to reserve life. God is angry with man because man destroys his own soul and self thus requiring God to render a just punishment on man. A punishment, a destruction in which God has no pleasure. Yet, because God is Justice, the Spirit of Justice must be fulfilled. To those who turn away from evil and accept God's mercy, His way of life, God has forgiveness, and, to those who reject God's way, He rewards them with suffering. They receive suffering because God takes away from around them all the love and peace that they rejected inside of them and God gives them an eternal existence without those comforts. God is a fair God. The wicked don't get to keep that which they had no true appreciation for, that which they took for granted.

Perhaps the religious joyfully receive these words because these words so clearly depict a sinner but the religious see themselves as saintly. However, I point to the Holy Scripture quoted at the start of this book. That which hath been is now. The question I deeply address in this book is, Are the Christians of today the same as the scribes and Pharisees of two-thousand years ago? Christians claim to represent the true way of God but is there understanding available to test them out? Will this understanding say, They say God guides them and has sent them, but He neither guides them nor sends them because they hear not Him, they know not His depths. I will show that the Spirit of Understanding has so said in times past and says nearly the same of many of these religious people today.

If this message has now dampened the joy of the religious, I assume then, that rank, blatant sinners rejoice in the religious' downfall.

Indeed, in the United States, today, there is much rank sinner rejoicing because the so-called religious right has been kicked out of government and the anti-moral, anti-religious crowd are in so-called power. Yet, the message in this book shall not cause these corrupted people to rejoice either, for the message here does not forsake one single moral or judicial principle contained in the Holy Scriptures, of which all sinners are condemned.

The reason why the Spirit of Understanding is supplying to speak against the religious is because they are *not* true carriers of the Word of God. They think simply reading, copying, imitating the print is actually *carrying* the Word of God. Myself, I prefer a parrot to them. The beautiful bird has more understanding, or at least not *inverse* understanding. But neither do Christians *believe* as fully as they claim to believe. Shallow worship, self-righteousness, hypocrisy, preferential treatment of persons based on wealth or other factors, shameless greed and grifting for money and also outright denial of parts of the Holy Scriptures have caused God to cast off the religious, even as He did in Christ's time or the time of the Babylonian Conquest.

That is why the religious persecuted the Holy Children of God, because God's holy servants foretold of the religious people's downfall, but the religious, being not of God, desperately tried to justify their failure. Saint Paul and Saint John also began to describe how that believers (but not doers) in Jesus Christ began to persecute them. I shall later present these Scriptures.

Jeremiah warned Israel that God would punish them for their wickedness but they raised themselves up false prophets and leaders that prophesied peace and deliverance, when there was none for them. Then they took Jeremiah and cast him into a deep pit, which *actually* reflected what they had done to the goodness in their own

～ BACKGROUND ～

souls! However, Jeremiah lived to sorrowfully see all those false leaders and their followers destroyed. The false prophets were presumptuous because they presumptuously used God's name and His Holy Scriptures to fulfill their own purpose. That which hath been is now.

> 10 Therefore will I give their wives unto others, and their fields to them that shall inherit them: for everyone from the least even unto the greatest is given to covetousness, from the prophet even unto the priest everyone dealeth falsely.
> 11 For they have healed the hurt of the daughter of my people slightly, saying, Peace, peace; when there is no peace.
> 12 Were they ashamed when they had committed abomination? Nay, they were not at all ashamed, neither could they blush: therefore shall they fall among them that fall: in the time of their visitation they shall be cast down, saith the Lord.
> (Jeremiah Chapter 8)

The religious have begun to fall, now, and there is no help for them because they do not love God with all their heart, soul, mind, and strength. Some may say that it is written in the Holy Scriptures that evil will destroy some of God's saints but they shall be resurrected. This is written and I believe it. However, are the religious not aware that God's holy servants were undefeatable, until such time that God chose for them to glorify Him by being persecuted and put to death for His Word, and, the holy children of God were willing to be so. By the way, being put to death for his Word is a *lot* more than parroting the Holy Scripture.

The holy children of God know when they are to leave this world and they accept it joyfully. Their sorrow is for others who have done wrong and bring upon themselves eternal destruction. Many times did the wicked try to put King David or Saint Paul to death but they could not, and so it is with all the holy children of God. However, when judgement is come upon the religious, many do not go to the grave willingly nor peacefully, and, when they see the grave approach, they cry out. But, it's too late. The holy children of God do no such dishonor to God because they *know* that God will keep them in peace until they are resurrected. They *know* because the presence of the Lord Jesus' Holy Ghost is continual in them. They do not sorrow over losing this world.

Look at all the religious in former Yugoslavia, the Christians, Muslims, and Jews. Are they terrified because of the wickedness on all sides? There are many other countries like this today. Many don't suffer willingly, nor do they go to the grave glorifying God because they know not the assurance of the Holy Spirit, because the Holy Spirit is not within them, nor even with them. It would be the same for those in any country because God is not with the religious, but with the holy.

The true children of God are rare, *holy* men and women, as Jesus said, Few there be that find it. But many of the religious *do* have the Holy Spirit dwelling *with them,* but it is there to help guide them to give their whole selves up to Jesus so that He can dwell *in them*. But they refuse to take that next step. Their faith is in *imitation* instead of being the real thing, holy from the inside out.

Christians believe they are saved simply because they *believe* Jesus is the Son of God, the Messiah. Can it be counted for belief if one believes ninety percent of God's Word and not the other ten percent? True, Abraham believed God and it was counted to him for righteousness, but *all* of God's words, for it is also written God said, 19 For I know him that he will command his children and his household after him, and they shall keep the way of the Lord, to do justice and judgement. (Genesis chapter 18) 5 Because that Abraham obeyed my voice and kept my charge, my commandments, my statutes, and my laws. (Genesis chapter 25)

In other words, Abraham believed and kept *all* of God's words and ways. His belief was verified by his actions because actions represent one's choices or belief of what is best to heed, they are the product of your heart, the fruit of your treasure. However, Christians believe they are saved merely because they believe Jesus is the Son of God. Yet, Jesus Himself went further and said,

> 21 Not everyone that saith unto me, Lord, Lord, shall enter into the kingdom of heaven; but he that doeth the will of my Father which is in heaven.
> 22 Many will say to me in that day, Lord, Lord, have we not prophesied in thy name? and in thy name have cast out devils? And in thy name done many wonderful works?
> 23 And then will I profess to them, I never knew you: depart from me, ye that work iniquity. (Matthew chapter 7)
> Yet Jesus also said,
> 29 This is the work of God, that ye believe on him whom He hath sent. (John chapter 6)

To *truly* believe on Jesus Christ means to believe and do *all* that Jesus said, not just do the things one likes to do, not just believe that He is the Son of God; for when one believes someone, one pays heed to all that he says. Also, a king does not count his subjects loyal if they recognize that the prince is the king's son but do not respect or follow his son's instructions. Believing on Jesus Christ is not just a recognition of His royal position, but it is being diligent to obey him in all that

He requests, since one knows that He is true and also has all power and authority. For those who feel I am overstressing the point, well, watch as the truth unfolds here, and see who is overstressing who!

The Pharisees who gave Jesus up to be crucified also had a very strong belief that God is real. Indeed, they also believed that God would send the Messiah, and they believed in the resurrection. So then, what difference is there between the Pharisees and today's Christians? Christians counter my point by saying, Yes, but the Jews didn't believe that Jesus was the Messiah, and, therefore, they are condemned because they believe not all of God's truth. The Jew's wickedness made their true belief in God to be of none effect. In response to all this, I therefore say to Christians that out of your own mouths and hearts shall you be judged because neither do Christians believe all of Jesus Christ's truth. Therefore, the Christians strong belief that Jesus is the Son of God is made of none effect. I shall prove this in this book! But *not* because I want to gloat over the Christian's failures, but because I want them to *wake up!*

The main point of my first book, What is in a Word, which shall be republished some time in the future, and the main point of this book is that God has always intended for people to live holy in *this* lifetime, as well as the life to come. To live holy can only mean living without sinning. This means that for a sinner to be truly saved, to truly believe Jesus Christ, he must seek God until he gets filled with the Holy Spirit, who keeps him from sinning. Surely this is being saved from sin, otherwise, what is salvation? Would not the Lord Jesus Chrit make salvation the product of His greatest love for us? Is not being transformed in *mortality* into holiness, a holiness that keeps us from sinning, is *that* not the greatest love Jesus could do for us? However, Satan has made many arguments against this belief in pure holiness on Earth, because people want to excuse their guilt, because they want an easy way to salvation, one that doesn't entail truly giving *all* of themselves to Jesus.

By disagreeing with pure holiness in mortality, those religious, so-called saved people, believe that as long as they exist in this lifetime, evil will always be able to conquer them, that is, to make them sin. To cover their lie of claiming that this wicked condition is salvation, they adopt the belief that God cannot make anyone perfect in this lifetime, even though one repents of *all* their sins and forsakes everything for Jesus Christ. I shall prove their arguments to be foolish and blasphemous. "The devil made me do it," is not an excuse that gets one into the kingdom of God, and, one who knows and believes God, and yet still turns away and sins is worse than those who don't know Him or believe Him. Even a rank sinner knows that! Religious *fools!*

But this is also why Jesus Christ came to Earth, to destroy Satan's boast that he ruled over every person on Earth and that they had to obey him. When Jesus Christ sacrificed Himself and then sent His Holy Ghost back to Earth, this destroyed evil's boast and showed Satan that he had no power on Earth either. Death is swallowed up in victory. Isn't what I just described a better victory than the lies Christians believe that no one can be perfect, therefore they have to keep sinning, or, well, you don't *have to*, but… you *will!* So sad! So sad that their faith is so weak, that they have believed lies that make sure to keep them weak.

I ask the foolish of their belief, When did God lose His power to make perfect beings or to restore that which is lost? When did Jesus Christ become so weak that His Holy Spirit could no longer resist evil in the flesh? And, when a person truly repents, how can one ask for anything less than perfection? To ask for anything less than perfection is to still hold onto some sin and then one cannot be forgiven. The command is to deny yourself, forsake *everything* for Jesus Christ, Let the Wicked forsake his way and the unrighteous man his thoughts and God will have mercy upon him. What mercy? Half mercy? Three-quarters mercy? Ninety-nine percent mercy?

I start my readers off by asking them to consider, when one is saved, isn't the same Spirit that is in Jesus Christ placed within the saved person? Didn't that Holy Spirit go through all trials and temptations and overcome them all without yielding to sin at all? How then should a truly saved person sin when this Holy Ghost of Jesus Christ is within that person? Before Jesus came, there was none able to continuously dwell perfectly on Earth, therefore, none of their images was able to save man from sinning. However, the image of Jesus Christ, which is the Holy Ghost, is able to make one perfect in *this* lifetime because Jesus dwelt here perfectly and will always be so.

CHAPTER 1

WHY DO CHRISTIANS BELIEVE THEY ARE SAVED?

I am delivering these words to the souls that have been tricked and misled by false leaders, and for many, many generations so that their worship is also tangled with family honor and respect. Important parts of life tangled together that should *not* be mixed together but false leaders also encourage this! Leaders who have absconded with the Holy Scriptures and used them to manipulate others unto their own purpose. This manipulation is religion. The Jews were never told to be Jewish but they created their own pride in it to which God responded telling them to be confounded for their own pride! However, the purpose of the holy printed word of God is already inherent within it and needs no doctoring, packaging, or family pride. One might ask, How can we do that when we are required to teach our children? By teaching them God is more important than anything and living it. By teaching them this isn't to please me, but to please God, for He is your life and your future. We pass away, God does not.

God's Word is Holy and eternal and its purpose is to bring forth and maintain the same, eternal holiness. God's word needs no fancy videos, no catchy tunes, no added jokes, no free gold pins, no family pride, or any other gimmick or device of the world to be mingled with it in order to attract souls. The calling of God's word is love, truth, and life, and the souls that love and seek God will respond to such a calling and no other. Why do you think that Jesus said, Whosoever loves father, mother, wife, husband, and other family more than Him is not worthy of Him, but even down to your own self, too!

However, those who mix the world up with that which is holy and then call themselves trying to 'win' souls for Christ are nothing but liars because the world attracts the souls that belong to the world and the truth of God draws the souls whom belong to God. And honor thy father and mother is owned by the Author of those commands, not the other way around where pride supplants what is most important. Therefore, to fulfill God's purpose one only needs to speak His Word by *His* Spirit and no other. God's word spoken, written, or sung in truth is sufficient and any addition is sacrilege. You might not realize it, but the writing, speaking, and singing of God's love does not use the world's format, but is given spontaneously by the Holy Spirit.

Unfortunately, there are other religious people who go too far in the other direction. They won't read this book because it is not the Bible and they *only* read the Bible. These people would *never* have listened to nor accepted Jesus Christ because Jesus brought new things, new words. These Bible thumpers put God in a box such that the Bible is their idol. Instead of worshiping the whole Tree of Life which is Jesus, they only want to deal with a tiny twig on that tree, and not the twig but the leaves thereon, where the printed word is. So sad.

To prove they reject the Holy Ghost, the paper and ink says the Holy Ghost will teach you *all* things, *whatsoever* Jesus said, and that

WHY DO CHRISTIANS BELIEVE THEY ARE SAVED?

is way more than what the Bible has, but all they do is thump the Bible as the end-all to end-all as if leaves can live without the whole tree. Try to have a conversation with any of these people which is based on Wisdom or Understanding, which are solid branches on the Tree of Life bringing forth an actual discussion, and all they can respond is that the Bible says. . .Therefore, they don't even understand nor follow the Holy Bible! They have become rotting dead leaves because, frankly, they can't even think, nor reason, and remember, reason cometh from God, from Wisdom! Unfortunately, the word *reason* has been demonized because they confuse yet other Scriptures which berate the reasoning of the world. This is even sadder, that they judge the Spirit of Wisdom as if He is worldly wisdom.

This book focuses on the differences between being holy and being religious. These are drastically different. Being holy is the continuous sanctification of a person by the Holy Spirit dwelling in that person, and, by virtue of this Spirit's consciousness and conscience, that person dwells by the same, that is, pureness, righteousness, love, wisdom, understanding, peace, justice, truth, joy, and eternal life. No sin or evil can dwell with this consciousness because all evil is rejected by the Holy Ghost and the new heart. No trick, manipulation, or so-called dark power can overcome Him because all power and knowledge are with the Holy Ghost and He protects the one in which He dwells. Therefore, whatsoever soul and body His Holy Spirit sanctifies, that person will not sin. Otherwise, sanctification would not be sanctification because sanctification is none other than being endowed with the qualities of the sanctifier. In other words, being made in God's image. A holy child of God. And, *no,* we are not slaves but very much have our own free will which is free to choose from an infinite, everlasting set of Goodness. It's not that we don't know that evil is there to choose. Satan tells us about it all the time! It's just that he doesn't interest us at all. Frankly, he's quite boring as well as all that he has to offer.

At this point the religious are calling *me* a devil, a blasphemer, and shouting to others not to listen. I've experienced this many times. No one can be perfect they say. Only *God* is perfect. How can you be perfect? Well, the first two statements are lies and not even Scriptural. In answer to the question, I shall explain: Our minds cannot be perfect, not right away. They address things point by point, mostly, and are unable to keep up with the intense assault of evil. However, didn't Jesus say all sin proceedeth from the heart? Not the mind. But *all* sin comes from the heart. The promise is that we are given a new heart, new spirit, which comes along with receiving the Holy Ghost and being born again. Think about it. When a child is born into the world, his heart is full, his mind is blank! Born *again,* you are given a new heart and new spirit but *not* a new mind. But the heart and spirit perceive en mass through feeling and sensing which is way past the mind's capabilities. So when any evil approaches, the new heart says NO, the new spirit says NO, and the mind is taught by them and learns, and is converted! Eventually, *every* thought and imagination is brought into captivity by the new heart and new spirit! Perfection indeed! Oh, also Scriptural, for those who make the Bible into their god!

I emphasize, there is no sin in God or His Holy Spirit, therefore, He cannot impute sin to His image, nor can He allow sin to exist within that heart, soul, mind, and body which is made of His image. Salvation, indeed. However, religion is *not* the Holy Spirit, therefore, religion has no power to sanctify. Moreover, religion has no consciousness, but is merely a construct of man to imitate or approximate

WHY DO CHRISTIANS BELIEVE THEY ARE SAVED?

things done by the Holy Spirit. In other words, all religion is a fake, a forgery. Why does one forge something? So that he can pass himself or his actions off as authentic when really he is a liar, an imposter.

To create the forgery, people use the Holy Scriptures to make an imitation of sanctification. Simply believe certain Scriptures, say a few selected words, give a certain amount of money, and oh, maybe cry a bit, some churches cry *a lot,* some relish in *intense* emotional displays, and then *finally,* religion sanctifies and saves you. One should be sure to continually give money if they want to remain saved. Saved from what? However, upon close examination of the forgery (religious doctrine) certain discrepancies appear. Certain lines of Scripture are left out. In fact, upon comparison of religious doctrine to the Holy Scriptures one can discern *major* omissions within religious doctrine. Therefore, a religious person lacks two things: The consciousness and conscience of the Holy Spirit dwelling *within* him, and the love and complete non-contradictory knowledge of the Holy Scriptures!

Now, every day there are people who, though well intentioned, are fooled by the counterfeiters and counterfeit currency. In their naiveté, trust, ignorance, and good intentions, they accept and receive counterfeit products. Many often discover the deception too late and suffer dire consequences. Many perceive the sleight-of-hand in one religion but then jump into another and there remain fooled! I write to all these people in hopes that they will not discover the truth too late.

Many fervently seek God through their religion, yet, when in the privacy of themselves, they look at themselves and feel a great lacking, something is missing, empty. At this point, the evil spirit gives them a thought, saying, You see? God isn't real. You're just making it up. I say, Ahh, how slick and tricky that evil spirit is. He mixed up a bit of truth with a big lie in hopes of baiting the person with the truth and causing him to swallow the lie. The truth is, Yes, man made up his religion and each individual manufactures feelings and acceptances to support the forgery because he believes it to be real. The big lie is what the evil spirit told him, God isn't real.

God is real. However, if one listens to the evil thought, one is carried even further into darkness. Evil says, The Bible is just made up. Now evil doesn't even have to overtly mix truth in with the lie. He's relying on one's acceptance of evil's first deception, that is, that one takes religion to be the same as God's way. Since one's conscience knows that his religion is manmade, he then can be tricked into thinking the Holy Scriptures were also manmade. Very tricky. However, one should always try to separate the lie from the truth. Fish often do this when they carefully clean the bait off a fisherman's hook without getting caught. The fish that do not clearly discriminate see the bait and the hook as one single delicacy and are pulled and tugged by the fisherman until they end up in the frying pan.

Often, people from one religion can see the mistakes or deceptions of another religion, but they cannot see their own. That is why evil has so many religions, so many different baits. Different people are blind to different tricks and wise to others. During the time that religious people begin to doubt what they are doing because God's Spirit through their conscience is showing them they're not right, the evil spirit is confusing them to think religion is God's way, that is, if the religious person doesn't believe the tricky thoughts of God isn't real, you're just making it up. But this is of no great matter to evil because evil has the first lie still waiting on the person: *religion*.

And this religion was the cause of the emptiness and consequent doubting of God in the first place. In response to the tricky thought, the religious person lies to himself, and says, No, God *is* real. I'm *not* making it up. But the word, *it,* refers to his religion as well as God, and hence maintains him in his self-deception. Then, if anyone tries to tell him that his religion isn't real, he runs from that truth like a fish who runs from a natural bait even if there is no hook in it! Religion makes people think they *cannot* approach God outside of any religious framework, therefore God without religion isn't safe, there *must* be a hook in Him somewhere! When the fish looks at the natural bait and supposed hook together, all he sees is hook and consequently concludes that all such bait is dangerous. Unfortunately, if that's the only food around for the fish then he is going to be one very hungry fish. So is the soul of a religious person who runs from the truth.

A religious person is caught in a net. Whether he tries to go up, forward, or backward, he is trapped, and, the more he moves the more tangled he gets. Hence the birth of either a religious zealot, an angry atheist, or your typical numbed every day religious folk! Since they're trapped in a net, they just stop moving, or they are like a hamster on a wheel constantly running but getting nowhere until they get bored enough to jump off. Evil uses a religious person's strongest feelings to push them one way or the other, between zealot or atheist, or convinces them that strong feelings are just in a *human* heart that they can't trust because only the Bible is worthy to be trusted. For those who do not have strong feelings for God or truth, evil doesn't worry about them. Evil is not going to lose their soul because they don't really care enough to love God or anything except immediate comforts of the world.

Undoubtably, there are many more kinds of religious people, who have no love for peace or truth, but who merely want a tool to oppress masses of people and give the oppressor a means of control, justification, and mastery. Since these people do not have any real feelings for God, I shall not too much concern myself with them in this book. I write to those religious and otherwise ignorant people, who truly have feelings for God, albeit mixed in with religion.

Look at how religion developed. Before a forgery can be produced, there has to be an original. God sent His Holy Word to man through His Holy Spirit within those whom He sanctified. Holy people. If His holy people began to resist God's will, God sorely chastised them for their own good, as Jonah was swallowed by the great fish and King David was cast out of Jerusalem and suffered the destruction of his children and kingdom. Never forget that though God gave us a free will and never forces us, that doesn't guarantee access to what we desire to choose from! The world around us can change at the blink of an eye.

It does not please God for man to try and mix sin in with holiness. That's why they were punished so severely. The Holy Spirit departed from them and they were left defenseless, to reap the rewards of the evil they sowed. Upon discovering their wickedness and vain existence, they sought forgiveness. However, it did not please God that His holy servants would step outside of God's way and so God swore to turn away *all* ungodliness from His servants so that they would never be ashamed any more, and, that, They will keep My commandments and do them, and, Their sin shall no longer be remembered. *That* is why Jesus Christ came and suffered, so that after He was risen from the grave , He could place that same upgraded Holy Spirit that is in Him, His Holy Ghost, within man to keep him from sinning. This Holy Spirit of the risen Jesus Christ conquered all sin and death by being tempted in all things, and, yet, not yielding to do evil, nor turning away at all from GOD, not even an unrighteous thought or an ungodly feeling. How else do you

WHY DO CHRISTIANS BELIEVE THEY ARE SAVED?

think the Scripture saying, Bringing into captivity *every* thought to the obedience of Christ, could be fulfilled? That is Paul describing to us what was actually happening in him!

When King David sinned, God replied to him, You have given great occasion for My enemies to blaspheme Me. Today, all religious people, *all* Christians also fulfill this occasion by still sinning, yet, claiming to be Jesus Christ's servants. Did Jesus send them to sin? The non-believers laugh and mock, Look at those hypocrite Christians. They *love* to sin just like us. Some God they have huh? Who needs a God like *that?* I think I'm more honest than those phony Christians. I don't claim to be saved when I enjoy *my* sinning. That's what they say. I've talked to many of them. Actually, they listen to the Spirit of Wisdom and Understanding far better than Christians when I speak to them!

Christian's pride will not want to hear this, but it is worse for Christians than for Jews before Christ, because Jesus Christ increased the power of the Holy Spirit through His overcoming all temptations while he was dwelling in the flesh. My strength is made *perfect* in weakness. In other words, Jesus tailor-made the Holy Ghost to keep man from sinning even while man is in the flesh and constantly buffeted by the evil spirit. This could not have been done without Jesus coming in the flesh and suffering within it. Therefore, man no longer has any excuse to sin! Since God and the Son of God suffered to ensure the continuous holiness, pureness, of His servants, isn't it a great provocation to now claim to serve God and, yet, still sin? With the Holy Ghost of Jesus Christ, one now has something with which to battle evil besides his own will and understanding, because the Holy Ghost is given to continuously abide *inside* man. Jesus said to his disciples,

And I will pray the Father, and He shall give you another Comforter, that he may abide with you forever. Even the Spirit of Truth. . . for he dwelleth with you, and shall be in you. . . But the Comforter, which is the Holy Ghost, whom the Father will send in my name, he shall teach you all things, and bring all things to your remembrance, whatsoever I have said unto you. (John chapter 14, verse 16, 17, 26)

Before Jesus came, the children of God only had their own will and the written word of God to battle evil. The Holy Spirit would come and go with the angels of God and man had to reserve their message after they departed. If the congregation as a whole did so, the Holy Spirit would also dwell in their midst! If King David, and other ancient servants of God before Christ, could have received the Holy Ghost that Jesus gave to God's servants after he rose from the grave, those ancient servants would not have stepped out from God at all. To know this for sure, all one has to do is look at the great faith they had in God, how they slew giants, defeated multitudes, parted waters, walked through the fiery furnace, overcame great wild beasts, and many other things they did because they believed God and knew Him. However, they were occasionally able to be tricked by the evil spirit because they were weak. The sacrifice of Christ, which is able to cleanse even our very consciences, hadn't been accessible in their lifetime. Yet, when they did sin, God punished them sorely.

I know there are those Christians who believe that Peter and other holy servants sinned even after they were filled with the Holy Ghost. However, these Christians are mistaken. They do not understand the few Holy Scriptures which on first *appearance* give such an impression. However, the deepness of the Spirit of Understanding reveals

WHY DO CHRISTIANS BELIEVE THEY ARE SAVED?

the truth of Peter and Paul's seeming contentions and also of Christ's chastisement of His holy servants in Revelations. We shall address it all in this book.

Today, Christians sin often, even at their own admission, but God doesn't trouble them as he did to those before Christ when His holy servants stepped wrong. Today, Christians seem to go unpunished. Why? Because they do not belong to God and His wrath is saved up for them and all the ungodly until Judgment Day. True, the Holy Spirit dwells *with* many Christians due to their *partial* faith that Jesus is the Son of God, but that's *not* enough, as the previous Scripture from John chapter 14 demonstrated.

God is very merciful and leaves the wicked and the sinners mostly alone to enjoy the little time they have, as David in the Psalms, Solomon in Ecclesiastes, and Job all testify about the prosperity of the wicked. However, the true children of God are plagued every day because Satan is trying to make them stumble. Also, the world simply hates the very presence of holy folks.

At least most of the Jews of today are not aware of who Jesus Christ really is. Christians blame them for the old hard-heartedness, overlooking the fact that Christians have not demonstrated anywhere near the glory of Jesus for the Jews to see *anything* Godly! So under these circumstances, the Jews of today cannot engage in blasphemy of the Holy Ghost that the Christians often display to a certain level! Jesus said the Holy Ghost would lead one into *all* truth, but Christians claim that the Holy Ghost does *not,* since they claim to be saved and yet still sin. Moreover, Christians do *not* believe the Holy Ghost leads them into all truth, they believe the Holy Bible, the *printed* word of God leads them! How much trust in the Holy Ghost is there in them if they trust the paper and ink more than the Holy Spirit?

THE FALL OF CHRISTIANITY

As Paul pointed out in chapter six of Romans, there are two kinds of salvation: The righteous are saved or free from sin, but the sinner is saved or free from righteousness.

> 18 Being then made free from sin, ye became the servants of righteousness... 20 For when ye were the servants of sin, ye were free from righteousness.

Well, if you don't trust the Holy Ghost to lead you into all truth, but put all your trust in Old Testament processes of trusting the *written* word of God, are you Christians not free from the new righteousness of Jesus Christ? Because you do *not* participate in the trust, faith, and inward process between your soul and the Holy Ghost within you. In fact, you don't have Him at all! You can't when you don't even trust the Holy Ghost! Now, is this not even *more* of a blasphemy than the current Jews do?

Unfortunately though, there are even some Jews who have taken up Christianity, so I also write to them in hopes that they shall see that Jesus did not tell anyone to be a Christian. He did say, Be perfect, and Peter reiterated that we are to be holy.

So, how did Christianity develop? How did the forgery get started? Remember, there were many Gentiles who believed that Jesus is the Son of God. The Holy Scriptures recount the following,

> And it came to pass, that while Appollos was at Corinth, Paul having passed through the upper coasts came to Ephesus: and finding certain disciples,
>
> 2 He said unto them, Have ye received the Holy Ghost since ye believed? And they said unto him, We have not so much as heard whether there be any Holy Ghost.

3 And he said unto them, Unto what then were ye baptized? (Acts chapter 19)

When those Gentiles heard that Jesus died so that He could send the Holy Ghost back to man to save him from sin and death, they believed and received, 6 . . . the Holy Ghost came on them; and they spake with tongues, and prophesied.

The truth that Jesus did, indeed, sacrifice his flesh and blood for the express purpose of sending the Holy Ghost back to man can be found in His testimony as follows, Jesus said,

7 Nevertheless I tell you the truth; it is expedient for you that I go away: for if I go not away, the Comforter will not come unto you; but if I depart, I will send him unto you. . .
12 I have yet many things to say unto you, but ye cannot bear them now.
13 Howbeit when he, the Spirit of truth, is come, he will guide you into all truth; for he shall not speak of himself; but whatsoever he shall hear, that shall he speak: and he will show you things to come.
14 He shall glorify me: for he shall receive of mine, and shall show it unto you.
(John chapter 16)

It is written in many places that many believed on Jesus' name. Yet, not all those who believed Jesus was the Son of God were saved, meaning filled with the Holy Ghost. Why? Because they did not do what Jesus told them they had to do in order to receive the Holy Spirit. I call to remembrance that there were many people that walked with Jesus when He was here, only to leave Him after a while because they

THE FALL OF CHRISTIANITY

could not accept the whole truth. 66 From that time many of his disciples went back, and walked no more with him. (John chapter 6)

As it was when Jesus was here on Earth, so also was it after He left and sent His holy servants to all nations. There were many believers in part, but not all of the truth. These partial believers were faced with a harsh reality: they believed part of the truth but not all of it and *that* just doesn't work psychologically, nor spiritually, certainly not philosophically. The parts they believed, they believed too strongly to let them go, but the parts they didn't believe troubled their conscience, knowing that if they didn't believe *all* the truth then they were finding fault with God and would be lost. They could not be saved without believing all the truth, neither could they enjoy the elevation of their conscience over the Jews, who were of old ordained as God's chosen people, whom the Gentiles long time envied, wondering, Why should God choose *them* and not *me*? But they saw their opportunity to say, Now God has chosen *us*.

Unfortunately, that envy and desire to now be elevated over those who for so long morally condemned them combined with the contradiction of believing only part of Jesus Christ's words. But add to that the persecution of Christians for the truth that they *did* believe and these combinations drove many of the Gentile Christians' consciences to be subverted to the forgery of religion. Their persecution focused their attention even more strongly on the righteousness that they *did accept,* but made it easier for them to forget or overlook the fact that they did not accept the whole truth of Jesus Christ. Hence the birth of the Christian religion. Oh, and the Jewish believers? Most of them were holy and done away with early on.

Religion, something that would elevate them in theirs and others' sight by reason of the truth they *do* believe, yet, justify them doing

WHY DO CHRISTIANS BELIEVE THEY ARE SAVED?

wrong by both changing and hiding those parts of the truth that condemn them. This statement is so true and accurate that I am sure it shall provoke considerable anger from those who haven't been able to completely destroy their consciences but yet still hold to religion. They don't like to perceive that they are wrong. Yet, how can they be truly saved if they don't both perceive it and seek to be free of the falsehoods? It is not my desire to provoke anger, but if that causes a soul to closer examine himself then I am satisfied with the end result.

Saint John's third letter attests to the religious situation by describing the following,

> 7 Because that for his name's sake they went forth, taking nothing of the Gentiles.
> 8 We therefore ought to receive such, that we may be fellow helpers to the truth.
> 9 I wrote unto the church: Di-ot 're-phes, who loveth to have the preeminence among them, receiveth us not.
> 10 Wherefore, if I come, I will remember his deeds which he doeth, prating against us with malicious words: and not content therewith, neither doth he himself receive the brethren, and forbideth them that would, and casteth them out of the church.
> 11 Beloved, follow not that which is evil, but that which is good. He that doeth good is of God: but he that doeth evil hath not seen God.

Note how in verse 10, the holy people are cast out of the church by the Christians, even as the holy people were cast out of the Holy Temple in the time before the Babylonian Conquest, or as when the Pharisees cast the holy out during Christ. The thing that hath been, it is that which shall be. . . That which hath been is now. . . and God requireth that which is past. See how the man, Dioptrephes, loves his preeminence in verse 9. This reminds me of how the wicked priests cast Jeremiah into a pit when they didn't like the word of God that was spoken through him. Yet, they died and went to Hell and Jeremiah was spared and laid his head down in peace.

Preeminence. Notice how that Diotrephes ruled in his church. It wasn't by the power of God but by malicious force, but he had many followers who felt he was righteous and the holy were not. Yet, when Paul was vexed by the ungodly, he glorified Jesus Christ by showing forth God's power, and said, The Lord Jesus Christ rebuke thee, and by the power of God one wicked man fell blind and the devil fled out from another. However, since the religious have very little, if any, power from God, they must use the forces of the ungodly world to achieve their protection and ends- man's weapons, craftiness, maliciousness, armies, enforcers, and collecting money. Oh yes, plenty of money. Yet, even when God sent His armies of the children of Israel out to battle, God was careful not to send too many, therefore delivering the multitudes of ungodly into the hands of a *few* holy people so that God should be glorified.

> 2 And the Lord said unto Gideon, The people that are with thee are too many for me to give the Midianites into their hands, lest Israel vaunt themselves against me, saying, Mine own hand hath saved me. Judges chapter 7)

This has always been God's way. God doesn't need nor use multitudes to do His will on Earth, thereby His power is glorified.

Religion came about from the multitudes of ungodly who loved part of God's truth but not all. Christians feel sure in their religion because they believe Jesus to be the Son of God and the Jews don't.

~ WHY DO CHRISTIANS BELIEVE THEY ARE SAVED? ~

This gives Christians a sense of preeminence much like the Jews have had because each has believed the truth that the other does not, yet, only the part that pleases themselves. They feel quite confident that they are saved and the unbeliever will go to Hell. I now record two of Paul's warnings to the Gentiles so that Christians will closely heed the message that follows in this book. So that they can believe *all* of the truth and not be wise in their own conceits.

> I say then, Hath God cast away his people? God forbid. For I also am an Israelite, of the seed of Abraham, of the tribe of Benjamin.
> 2 God hath not cast away his people which he foreknew. Wot ye not what the Scripture saith of Elijah? How he maketh intercession to God against Israel, saying,
> 3 Lord, they have killed thy prophets, and digged down thine altars: and I am left alone, and they seek my life.
> 4 But what saith the answer of God unto him? I have reserved to myself seven thousand men, who have not bowed the knee to the image of Baal.
> 5 Even so then at this present time also there is a remnant according to the election of grace.
> 6 And if by grace, then is it no more of works: otherwise grace in no more grace. But if it be of works, then is it no more grace: otherwise work is no more work.
> 7 What then? Israel hath not obtained that which he seeketh for; but the election hath obtained it, and the rest were blinded.
> 8 (According as it is written, God hath given them the spirit of slumber, eyes that they should not see, and ears that they should not hear;) unto this day.

9 And David saith, Let their table be made a snare, and a stumbling block, and a recompense unto them:

10 Let their eyes be darkened, that they may not see, and bow down their back alway.

11 I say then, Have they stumbled that they should fall? God forbid: but rather through their fall salvation is come unto the Gentiles, for to provoke them to jealousy.

12 Now if the fall of them be the riches of the world, and the diminishing of them the riches of the Gentiles; how much more their fulness?

13 For I speak to you Gentiles, in as much as I am the apostle of the Gentiles, I magnify mine office:

14 If by any means I may provoke to emulation them which are my flesh, and might save some of them.

15 For if the casting away of them be the reconciling of the world, what shall the receiving of them be, but life from the dead?

16 For if the first fruit be holy, the lump is also holy: and if the root be holy, so are the branches.

17 And if some of the branches be broken off, and thou, being a wild olive tree, wert grafted in among them, and with them partakest of the root and fatness of the olive tree;

18 Boast not against the branches. But if thou boast, thou bearest not the root, but the root thee.

19 Thou will say then, The branches were broken off, that I might be grafted in.

20 Well; because of unbelief they were broken off, and thou standeth by faith. Be not highminded, but fear:

21 For if God spared not the natural branches, take heed lest he also spare not thee.
22 Behold therefore the goodness and severity of God: on them which fell, severity; but toward thee, goodness, if thou continue in his goodness: otherwise thou also shall be cut off.
23 And they also, if they abide not still in unbelief, shall be grafted in: for God is able to graft them in again.
24 For if thou wert cut out of the olive tree which is wild by nature, and wert grafted contrary to nature into a good olive tree: how much more shall these, which be the natural branches, be grafted into their own olive tree?
25 For I would not, brethren, that ye should be ignorant of this mystery, lest ye should be wise in your own conceits; that blindness in part is happened to Israel, until the fullness of the Gentiles be come in.
26 And so all Israel shall be saved: as it is written, There shall come out of Sion the Deliverer, and shall turn away ungodliness from Jacob:
27 For this is my covenant unto them, when I shall take away their sins. . .
(Romans chapter 11)

Saint Paul warned the Gentiles much like Moses warned Israel, yet, not Moses or Paul, but the Holy Spirit speaking through them. In order for the Jews to have failed God, they had to ignore the word of God that was taught to them and break God's law. It was important for all of them, together, and of their own will, to keep all God's law, otherwise they would fail because they were weak, the Holy Ghost of Jesus Christ having not been accessible to them before Christ. However, now, in order for the Jews or Gentiles to fail, they have to not receive the Holy Ghost, because the Holy Ghost does not fail. One who is filled with the Holy Ghost has denied himself, his own will, for God's will, and is not of himself, but the Father that is in him does the works. So I give my readers a small portion of the warning that Moses issued,

> 28 Gather unto me all the elders of your tribes, and your officers, that I may speak these words in their ears, and call heaven and earth to record against them.
>
> 29 For I know that after my death ye will utterly corrupt yourselves, and turn aside from the way which I have commanded you; and evil will befall you in the latter days; because ye will do evil in the sight of the Lord, to provoke him to anger through the work of your hands. (Deuteronomy chapter 31)

After the last elders of Israel had died, whom had known and seen the glorious works of God, then the children of Israel left from serving God and rebelled against Him. Also, after Paul had left the Gentiles, false teachers came and hid the beautiful holy way that God had made accessible to them. They hid the knowledge of the Holy Ghost and of receiving it. That is the only way that evil could keep the Gentiles from continuing in the ways of Jesus Christ. Paul also warned as follows,

> 17 And from Miletus he sent to Ephesus, and called the elders of the church. . .
>
> 25 And now, behold, I know that ye all, among whom I have gone preaching the kingdom of God, shall see my face no more.
>
> 26 Wherefore I take you to record this day, that I am pure from the blood of all men.

WHY DO CHRISTIANS BELIEVE THEY ARE SAVED?

27 For I have not shunned to declare unto you all the counsel of God;
28 Take heed therefore unto yourselves, and to all the flock, over the which the Holy Ghost hath made you overseer, to feed the church of God, which he has purchased with his own blood.
29 For I know this, that after my departing shall grievous wolves enter in among you, not sparing the flock.
30 Also of your own selves shall men arise, speaking perverse things, to draw away disciples after them.
31 Therefore watch, and remember, that by the space of three years I ceased not to warn everyone night and day with tears.
(Acts chapter 20)

Just as many of the Jews fell and were destroyed, yet, a holy remnant were saved, so also does it now happen to the Gentiles and only the holy shall be saved; for God is long suffering and willing to let the world fall into utter darkness for the sake of the few souls that still turn away from such darkness and become holy. In Noah's time God held the whole world together to save just eight souls. Yet, God gave the world warning, though they would not pay heed. However, I specifically address this book to Christians because they falsely claim to represent Jesus Christ and are thereby a stumbling to those who seek in earnest for the Living God. As it happened to the Jews, so also does it happen to the Christians, The thing that hath been, it is that which shall be; That which hath been is now. Jesus said the following,

13 But woe unto you, scribes and Pharisees, hypocrites! for ye shut up the kingdom of heaven against men: for ye neither go

in yourselves, neither suffer ye them that are entering to go in. (Matthew chapter 23}

52 Woe unto you, lawyers! For ye have taken away the key of knowledge: ye entered not in yourselves, and them that were entering in ye hindered.

53 And as he said these things unto them, the scribes and the Pharisees began to urge him vehemently, and to provoke him to speak many things:

54 Laying wait for him, and seeking to catch something out of his mouth, that they might accuse him. (Luke chapter 11)

7 He that overcometh shall inherit all things; and I will be his God, and he shall be my son.

8 But the fearful, and unbelieving, and the abominable, and murderers, and whoremongers, and sorcerers, and idolators, and all liars, shall have their part in the lake which burneth with fire and brimstone: which is the second death. (Revelation chapter 21)

CHAPTER 2

WHICH RELIGION? SILVER AND GOLD HAVE I NONE

There will be no contradictions in this book. If my readers find what appears to be a contradiction, feel free to contact me and explain where and why you think there is a discrepancy. By the grace of God, I will answer you back. You can find me on X, former Twitter.

Many people believe there to be contradictions in the Holy Bible. This is because they do not understand what they read. There are no contradictions in the Holy printed Word of God. That is impossible, because, as God said, Hear Oh Israel, the Lord our God, the Lord is One. And Jesus said, I and my Father are One. The words that I speak unto you I speak not of myself: but the Father that dwelleth in me, He doeth the works.

If there was a contradiction anywhere in the Holy Word of God then there would be two opposing principles. That would indicate that God would not be One, but divided against Himself. However, as Jesus pointed out, God is One but Satan is divided against himself. Look at how many religions there are today. There are so many different Christian religions, each disagreeing and contradicting the other in many points. Does not this situation alone show people to whom the religions belong? Not God. Besides conflicting with each other, the religious also have in common the same core self-contradictory doctrine that I am pointing out in this book. However, the holy people, which now come from every nation, are not divided because the God they serve is One God, the God of Truth. However, the god of liars has many different ways to follow him because a lie twists and changes according to the desires of evil. What did Paul say about this?

> 10 Now I beseech you, brethren, by the name of our Lord Jesus Christ, that ye all speak the same thing, and that there be no divisions among you; but that ye be perfectly joined together in the same mind and in the same judgment.
> 11 For it hath been declared unto me of you, my brethren, by them which are of the house of Chloe, there are contentions among you.
> 12 Now this I say, that every one of you saith, I am of Paul; and I of Apollos; and I of Cephus, and I of Christ.
> 13 Is Christ divided? Was Paul crucified for you? or were you baptized in the name of Paul? (1Corinthians chapter 1)
> 3 For ye are yet carnal: for whereas there is among you envying, and strife, and divisions, are ye not carnal, and walk as men?
> 4 For while one saith, I am of Paul: and another, I am of Apollos; are ye not carnal?
> (1Corinthians chapter 3)

Let me see. There are Protestants, Catholics, Baptists, Lutherans, Methodists, Jehovah's Witnesses, Seventh Day Adventists, Unitarians, Episcopals, Presbyterians, Jewish Messianic Christians, orthodox, conservative, reformed, and reconstructionist. Within many of these there are also many divisions such as American Baptists, Free Will Baptists, Independent Baptists, and Southern Baptists. I don't think there are any Northern Baptists, though, But, I am sure there are many more religious divisions and divisions of the divisions and divisions of those. Jesus said,

> But I know you, that ye have not the love of God in you.
> 43 I am come in my Father's name, and ye receive me not: if another shall come in his own name, him ye will receive. (John chapter 5)

The only way to glorify God and to serve Him is to be filled with His Holy Spirit. The Holy Spirit does not disagree with Himself, as Paul's Scripture admonishes, saying, . . . be perfectly joined together in the same mind and in the same judgment. The only way this is possible is to deny oneself, pick up his cross, and get filled with the Holy Ghost so that one can be led by Jesus Christ. Otherwise, how can one follow Jesus if he is not led by His Holy Ghost? However, there are many Christians who believe that the Holy Spirit does disagree against Himself and that there are places in the Holy Bible that portray this. I shall address these false accusations in this and my next book, God's Creative Writing, which is already in print. But now I shall continue to address the downfalls of religion and more testimony of what it is to be holy.

Ask most people about an obvious flaw with religious officers and they will say the unquenchable appetite for money. It seems that they believe that without that stuff, they cannot serve God. If one does not give them money then that *stingy* person is guilty of holding back God's work, the religious claim. However, if the religious are not truthfully representing Jesus Christ to the world, then those who do give them money are not furthering God's will but the devil's will. This is why it is written, Jesus said,

> 21 Not everyone that saith unto me, Lord, Lord, shall enter into the kingdom of heaven; but he that doeth the will of my Father which is in heaven.
> 22 Many will say to me at that day, Lord, Lord, have we not prophesied in thy name? and in thy name cast out devils? And in thy name done many wonderful works?
> 23 And then will I profess unto them, I never knew you: depart from me, ye that work iniquity. (Matthew chapter 7)

They didn't get filled with the Holy Ghost. They believed the lies that kept them from it. They believed the lies because those lies were their truth! Or should I say, the lies are their true nature which they identified with. They did all those good works just because they could do them, not because Jesus sent them. Feeding the hungry, clothing the naked, and healing the sick, yet, all the while spreading false doctrine and making sure there is enough money for their own selves to lavishly dwell. Therefore, they do not glorify God.

The holy children of God do not ask for money to do God's work. Neither do they accept a salary for being Jesus Christ's servant. When the people took up a collection for the saints at Jerusalem, they were not asked or compelled to do so. It was of their own free will and Paul only sought for an expedient way to send their gift. It did not please Paul to put his own hand to the money and asked that someone be appointed to carry it. Neither did he accept any for himself, lest his own ministry should have a blemish from people's accusations that he preached to them to receive their money. However, the false preachers of today preach to an audience and receive from that same audience, often in the same hour, a monetary reward. But Paul said,

> Now concerning the collection for the saints, as I have given order to the churches of Galatia, even so do ye.
> 2 Upon the first day of the week let every one of you lay by him in store, as God has prospered him, that there be no gatherings when I come.
> 3 And when I come, whomsoever ye shall approve by your letters, them will I send to bring your liberality unto Jerusalem. (1Corinthians chapter 16)

Notice that Paul said, That there be no gatherings when I come. He remembered what Jesus did when Jesus whipped and scourged the money-changers and drove them out of the temple, saying, My house shall be called an house of prayer for all people, but ye have made it a den of thieves. Paul did not want to make merchandise of his ministry, neither did he want to rob the people by exchanging for money that which he did not own, namely the Gospel of Jesus Christ. Notice also that the money was to be sent to others far away and Paul would not receive any of it nor so much as put his hand upon it. To further convince my readers that the children of God do not take reward, I cite further Scripture,

> 33 I have coveted no man's silver, or gold, or apparel.
> 34 Yea, ye yourselves know, that these hands have ministered unto my necessities, and to them that were with me.
> 35 I have showed you all things, how that so laboring ye ought to support the weak, and to remember the words of the Lord Jesus, how he said, It is more blessed to give than to receive. (Acts chapter 20)

Notice that Paul worked with his hands to support himself and the brethren that were with him, as God commanded from the beginning to Adam that he should get his living by the sweat of his brow. Notice also that Paul gives to the people and *they* receive. Now if Paul were to accept recompense from the people for what he gave unto them, then his giving is no longer giving, but selling or exchanging the Gospel for worldly gain. However, Paul speaks even more boldly against accepting carnal rewards for spiritual gifts,

> 11 If we have sown unto you spiritual things, is it a great thing that we should reap your carnal things?
> 12 If others be partakers of this power over you, are not we rather? Nevertheless we have not used this power; but suffer all things, lest we should hinder the gospel of Christ. . .
> 15 But I have used none of these things: neither have I written these things, that it should be so done unto me: for it were better for me to die, than that any man should make my glorying void. . .
> 18 What is my reward then? Verily that, when I preach the gospel, I may make the gospel of Christ without charge, that I abuse not my power in the gospel.
> (1 Corinthians chapter 9)

I recall how that Elijah went to the poor widow and asked for her last bit of oil and flour. She, through great faith in God, though she and her son were about to perish from starvation, made her last cake and gave it to the man of God, for the Spirit of God spoke through Elijah saying that her barrel of flour and cruse of oil would not go empty during the famine, and it was so. The point I am making is that the children of God do not burden people nor put them in hardship.

However, the religious will take a woman's last dime and tell her to bear the hardship because it is God's will, and, that she can expect a miracle, for complying. However, no blessing comes to her from this action because she helped further a false leader.

Just the other day I was listening to one of those so called great television preachers. I noticed that their tricks are becoming more and more devious as time passes. He told the congregation that God wanted them to be financially independent so that they could go out and do God's work. He also told them about Elijah and the widow woman's faith and how she gave everything she had to the man of God. The false leader thereby conned much money from people. I myself, was burning with the anger of the Spirit of Justice from Christ because of the hypocrisy and utter callousness of that liar on television. What about *him* being financially independent? Is he financially independent or living off what he swindles out of naïve people? When the widow woman helped Elijah, she immediately received compensation. However, the type of financial independence that liar on television was describing was the making of other people's finances to be independent of their pocketbooks and placed in his.

I also bring to remembrance how many times when evening came, that Jesus Himself, went to continue on further, rather than stay at someone's home and burden them during mealtime. The people had to greatly constrain Him for Him to dine with them. This is in stark contrast to many of those Sunday morning preachers who inform Sister Rose or Brother Harry that he will grace their tables with his insatiable appetite, and when he dines, he not only savors the food but also its feminine preparer.

Or, some false preachers just wander the neighborhood to see whom they can compel through guilt to heap sustenance upon them.

Many neighbors say, "Oh, look out. Here comes that preacher again to see if he can get some of my chicken." Her friend will say, "It's our God given duty." But the other answers back, "If he wants to be fed, let him work for it like everyone else. I don't see that he glorifies God so much by the way he acts." When Jesus accepted charity from someone, it was not through a trick , compulsion, or guilt that He received their gift. It was from their own unsolicited love and free will offering. Does this sound like religious leaders today?

When you sit in your churches and the basket comes around do you feel like your prayers will be answered if you *don't* drop in the money? But then, are you *buying* your prayer answers from God? They tell you that your offering will be rewarded. So, are you then exchanging money for your reward? Is *that* the way it really works? Let's see!

I ask my readers to forgive my redundancies. If in fact I am repetitious, it cannot be comparable to the repeated violation of people and God's ways by the religious, thus requiring me to present a substantial rebuke of such long entrenched pernicious ways. I further record Paul's justification,

> 14 Behold the third time I am ready to come unto you; and I will not be burdensome to you: for I seek not yours, but you: for the children ought not to lay up for the parents, but the parents for the children.
>
> 15 And I will very gladly spend and be spent for you; though the more abundantly I love you, the less I be loved.
>
> 16 But be it so, I did not burden you: nevertheless, being crafty, I caught you with guile.
>
> 17 Did I make a gain of you by any of them whom I sent unto you?

> 18 I desired Titus, and with him I sent a brother. Did Titus make a gain of you? walked we not in the same spirit? Walked we not in the same steps? (2Corinthians chapter 12)

I point out Saint John's third epistle, Because that for his name's sake they went forth, taking nothing of the Gentiles (verse 7) Holy people do not take reward nor can they be paid to preach God's word. Why? Because the word of God is preached strictly for His name's sake, which sake is eternal salvation. God's work is not done for the sake of collecting money, not even for 'earning' a living. However, today, all religions have their money organizers, who in turn pay this one to preach and that one to teach, hire and fire this one and that one. Yet, the real holy people are neither hired nor fired by man concerning God's work. Jesus Christ is holy people's reward and Jesus sends them out any time, any place, to preach his gospel.

Ask yourselves a serious question, Would you let someone like me stand up in the midst of your congregation and speak as the Holy Ghost gives me to speak? Oh my goodness, let me stop laughing. No, you would not. The Holy Ghost is not approved by your leaders to speak nor would he be appreciated like that. But isn't that *exactly* what Jesus did in the synagogues?

In summation of the matter of God's servants situation, I record Peter and John's testimony to the people,

> Now Peter and John went up together into the temple at the hour of prayer, being the ninth hour.
> 2 And a certain man lame from his mother's womb was carried, whom they laid daily at the gate of the temple which is called Beautiful, to ask alms of them that entered into the temple;

THE FALL OF CHRISTIANITY

> 3 Who seeing Peter and John about to go into the temple asked an alms.
> 4 And Peter, fastening his eyes upon him with John, said, Look on us.
> 5 And he gave heed unto them, expecting to receive something of them.
> 6 Then Peter said, Silver and gold have I none; but such as I have give I thee: In the name of Jesus Christ of Nazareth rise up and walk.
> 7 And he took him by the right hand, and lifted him up: and immediately his feet and ankle bones received strength.
> 8 And he leaping up stood, and walked, and entered with them into the temple, walking and leaping, and praising God. (Acts chapter 3)

Amazing isn't it? All that praising and rejoicing and never a penny exchanged hands. How can that be? I say to the religious leaders, listen close to what James wrote in chapter 5,

> Got to now, ye rich men, weep and howl for your miseries that shall come upon you.
> 2 Your riches are corrupted, and your garments are motheaten.
> 3 Your gold and silver is cankered; and the rust of them shall be a witness against you, and shall eat your flesh as it were fire. Ye have heaped treasure together for the last days.

Why don't you so called church leaders and so called church preachers be honest? Honest with yourselves and your people. God didn't send you, nor did Jesus, nor did the Holy Ghost. All you've done is feel like you wanted a *career* doing what you are doing. You went to school. Taught by other *men*. Your sermons are *rote*, regurgitated day after day, year after year from the Bible and other books of *men* you study. You strain to make them all sound new after about the first year on the job. They are like *college* lectures, often complete with study guides. *If* you were honest, you would tell everyone, Look, God didn't send *any* of us. But we really like what we're doin' studyin' the Bible. Discussin' it a bit. Lauding other men's books. Sounding wise when we aren't. Hey, maybe someone accidently gets helped by us. And it's worth paying us to do this. And look, I know this whole religion thing is now failing *miserably*, because the Beast is rising now and we don't have any power to stand against him *at all*. After all, we aren't *holy* like those legendary folks in the Bible. And truly, it's mainly because of Christians' *failures* that the Beast is rising now and destroying our children faster than we can get them baptized, not that baptism matters that much because it's only a *symbol* of what we call faith.

See how easy it is to tell the truth? Oh, by the way, the Lord Jesus has had me to baptize a bit. It's *not* a symbol. And those that actually go under right, and get filled with the Holy Ghost under there, well, they can tell you what it's *really* like to be truly born again. You see, you can't breathe under that water. No. And *all* you ever did in this mortal life, you did with your breathing life, right? So, if you *truly* want to give your whole life up to Jesus, when you go under there, *after the Lord has prepared you to go under there and showed you also what part of His presence He will send you under there*, well, once you can't breathe under the water then you don't worry about it! Because you truly aren't interested in your mortal life any more. (See how you immediately start to doubt this? It proves you are all liars.) You want to give your whole *damned* mortal life back under that water, *true* repentance. How are you gonna do that if you *fear? Fear for your condemned mortal life.*

Now, it is a *unique* experience from that point on for each individual but here is one way it can go: And after certain processes take place under that water and you've given all of yourself that you think you have under there, and the Lord Jesus' presence comes close, closer than ever before, well, by his Light shining upon you like never before, you're gonna see the *rest* of what you need to give up of yourself! Because you couldn't see it until that closer Light showed it to you. And *then* when you look into the presence of Jesus and say, Well, I don't want that part of myself either, all I want is you, Lord Jesus. And you open up fully to his presence, well, when you've done that completely, then you receive His presence faster than you would ever believe! You will *experience* that, and it ain't just with your five senses. No! In fact, your experience has nothing to do with your five senses. And then you don't want to come up from under that water even though you don't even know how long you've been under there! Depends upon how long it takes you to complete the process. If it's a holy person holding you under the water, they will know when to bring you up. Well, if it's *not* a holy person, well, you are on your own, but he'll probably just dunk ya pretty quick, in and out. It's that easy. And then tell you that you are saved! And the lie repeats, and repeats, and repeats. . .

CHAPTER 3

FAITH, GRACE, WORKS, AND RELIGIOUS CONFUSION

As I mentioned before, there are different religions because different people are blind to different portions of God's Truth. Now, many generations later, instead of praying and asking God for His meaning and Understanding of His Word, people still use their own mind and puny understanding to try to figure out God's message. Actually, they do this not to find out what God means, but to fit His printed word into their *own* meaning. Shame, shame on them.

In order for the religious to make their interpretations more believable, they go to, so called, great learned people. People who have certifications from great places of man's learning. What did Jesus say about these great places?

> Ye are they which justify yourselves before men; but God knoweth your hearts: for that which is highly esteemed among men is abomination in the sight of God. (Luke chapter 16, verse 15)

What do the holy children of God need with man's schools? Are these religious schools better able to teach a person than the Holy Ghost of Jesus Christ? Did Jesus Christ say that in order to get filled with the Holy Ghost, man must go to a religious school, or any school? Also, religious people consult other men's books and language consultants and historians, and interpreters, trying to figure out exactly what even a single word means in the Holy Scriptures. This is about as foolish as those fools who try to discover the secret of Creation of life by examining the lifeless, inanimate dust of the Earth and its lifeless inanimate principles. *Conscious life* doesn't come from dead, inanimate dust and neither does knowledge and understanding come from the ignorant and foolish. They come from the Omniscient, Omnipotent, Omnipresent Living God. I ask the religious a question, What's the matter, did God forget what His own words mean? Is this what the religious believe and therefore the reason they consult other men and not God concerning the meaning of God's word? Or, do the religious have no faith? In fact, the non-religious know you don't have any faith, that you're not real and that's why they don't bother with you. Jesus said,

> And they shall be all taught of God. Every man therefore that hath heard, and hath learned of the Father, cometh unto me. (John chapter 6, verse 45)

Jesus did say, come unto Him. Why then do the religious consult and trust other men more than the Living God? Some will say, But the written word was given to us to consult instead of having to bother God all the time. Well, if God's Word had a place in their hearts then they would understand it and would not have to consult their own or other minds concerning it. Therefore, their delusion is made strong, because they seek themselves and not God's Truth only. This comes

FAITH, GRACE, WORKS, AND RELIGIOUS CONFUSION

to pass that they should *not* have inheritance with the holy children of God, even as Paul described concerning the Pharisees. The holy word of God is a help to those who truly seek him and a stumbling to those who don't. That which hath been is now.

What is faith? Is it just a belief with no effect? What is the difference between a faith in a falsehood and a faith in Truth? To understand the answer to these questions is to understand why Paul emphasizes faith and James emphasizes works, yet, both are in agreement! To not understand the Holy Scriptures brings about confusion, different religions, wars, and abominations.

When one has faith in something, what are its conditions and how does faith effect that person? True faith first entails knowledge and understanding. One *knows* in what or in whom his faith is placed. From this knowledge comes the understanding that the object of one's faith will recompense or respond according to certain principles. A carpenter trusts his nails to maintain their strength and straightness even though he forcefully drives them into the wood. When one prays to God, he trusts that God will answer because he knows God is Love, Almighty, and will always be so. His innate nature is unchangeable.

Since a carpenter trusts the qualities of his nails, this trust enables him to order his actions around this trust. He does not inspect each nail, neither is he tentative about grasping and driving nail after nail in rapid succession . If he was doubtful about their quality, he would not be able to finish the house he's building because too much time would be taken in testing each nail and too much energy would be lost over the constant worry produced by his doubt. His will to build the house would be undermined. Eventually, he would give up his task because his faith in the *failure* of the nails is greater than his faith in their adequacy. His faith in failure is rewarded by same.

Likewise, when one has faith in the ever-loving ever-living Almighty God, this enables one to order his thoughts and ways around Love, Peace, Understanding, and many other qualities of God. Even though the totality of God is beyond man's full comprehension, a smidgen of an encounter with the Spirit of God is enough to produce the needed knowledge and understanding to instill faith and trust toward God within that person. The results of this are that a faithful person is not fearful or worried by evil's trials and temptations of him. Indeed, the more he is tested, the stronger becomes his faith because every temptation that is overcome is verification and an added surety to his faith. In this overcoming he turns even closer to the source of his faith, and the question, How much do you love Me, is repeatedly answered.

God allows all this for our own sakes, that we should know that we love God more than anything else and thus His knowledge and glory is magnified to and within us. Whether it be joyfully receiving rebukes and scorns for Christ's name's sake or denying one's own self-indulgence in the many lustful pleasures of the world in order to preserve ones integrity, or, the ultimate test of facing death for His Truth, the overcoming of these is done by faith in who and what God is. That brings to a person an ever increasing appreciation for God.

God is Love and He is Holy and that is the only way one can have eternal life, because there is an unblemished integrity in Holy Love. Therefore, there is unblemished integrity in the holy love which God may place in a person. Therefore, because God wants us to live, when one seeks His way of Life, God responds by placing holy love in that person, God's ever living image. In this manner one's body becomes the instrument of God's undefiled love because the Holy Ghost has power over all flesh.

~ FAITH, GRACE, WORKS, AND RELIGIOUS CONFUSION ~

However, a sinner uses the soul of life for the sake of pleasing his body. The body dies and so does the sake of the body. Thus, the sinner dies because he makes his soul to be for the sake of his body. That is his choice and he doesn't have to fight for the right to go to Hell. All who want to go to Hell only have to choose to go there and there is always room, (Pro-Choice, Pro-choice).

A holy person lives because God made his body for the sake of his soul. His body may be destroyed, yet, the sake of his soul lives and for God's holy child's soul's sake, his body shall be resurrected unto the eternal life of his soul.

Yet, the sinner is also resurrected for the sake of the corruption of his body and soul and thus suffers eternal suffering and destruction, because he caused God's life that was in him to suffer and corrupted himself for the sake of destroying the ways of God. The sinner has faith in his corrupted flesh and his faith is rewarded by that eternal destruction. For corruption is destruction, and God rewards every faith and sake that man has by giving him the fruits thereof to eternally fulfill his choices. Everyone has faith and everyone's faith is rewarded accordingly.

What happens, though, if the carpenter has a foolish faith such as believing he can drive his eight-penny nails through granite or steel plate? The result is that he drives in vain. So also do Christians drive in vain. How so?

A Christian's faith is this, Even though I must die a sinner, I will be rewarded by God with everlasting life. Even though, I, a Christian, do not love and serve God with *all* my heart, soul, mind, and strength, God will say, That's O.K. You're just human. I'm going to give you what you didn't want, that being perfect eternal life and holiness.

If the Christian's faith were really true then Satan himself would be saved! However, it is well known that Satan cannot be saved. Neither can Christians be saved as long as they be Christians and not holy children of God *only*. Satan does what seems good to himself, yet, before God there is no goodness in him. So also do Christians do what seems good to themselves. However, the prayer to God is, Thy will be done, not my will. There is no sin in God's will. Christians claim to be of God's will, yet, they also believe and admit that they will continue to sin until they die. They often remind each other, we are all sinners. And they *don't* mean it in the distant *past* tense, otherwise, why do they in their churches keep repenting every Sunday? What, do they keep repenting for their past sins *before* they became Christians? So, what, they didn't mean it enough the Sunday before? No. They keep repenting because they keep sinning.

Therefore, Christians do not worship Jesus Christ! The god that Christians worship does not exist except in their own minds because they worship a god that supposedly is all Love and Goodness, yet, will force them to be something they don't want to be. They think God is going to make them holy after they die when they chose to be a sinner when they died. However, the God of Love does not force nor tamper with the free will He gave to man. If one wants to die a sinner, that is his choice and God does not change man's choice or his reward for his choice.

If God tampered with man's free will, He would be lying because the will that God called free would not be free. Neither would anyone be justly punished because if God would tamper with one person's will, He would have to tamper with all wills, thus making God, not people, responsible for all their actions. But God never forces anyone because Love never forces. A just and loving God doesn't show preferences between persons, as Scriptures says, *Everyone* shall be judged according to the work of *their* hands. Respect not the person of the

~ FAITH, GRACE, WORKS, AND RELIGIOUS CONFUSION ~

rich, nor poor, but in righteousness shalt thou judge. Therefore, God does not tamper with even one person's free will.

Love cannot be Love without being Just, unless you think you can tell your loved ones you love them unjustly. All this is why God does not tamper with man's free will and lets man choose death. God's Love is One with Justice. The very reason why man is judgable is because he has a free will to try to do whatever he chooses.

Jesus said that in order to serve Him and be resurrected into eternal life, one must deny himself, forsake *everything* for Him and pick up his cross and follow Him. If a Christian claims to have denied himself completely for God and then still sins, is he then ascribing sin to God, since his self is denied and replaced by a new heart and new spirit with the Holy Ghost leading one into *all* truth? Or, is the Christian just a liar, since sin is of one's self and not of God? It is self and self-will that causes one to sin. That is why man is required to deny himself. If one chooses to completely deny his self for God's will, then only God's will shall be done in him, for he faithfully asked to receive the Holy Ghost (the Holy Ghost being God's will) to be made in God's image. After receiving the Holy Ghost there is nothing within that holy person to compel him to sin.

Once a person is holy, his free will choices become different from a sinner's choices. A holy person chooses to follow the Holy Ghost that is within him rather than follow the ungodly world that is outside of him. The sinner who tries to be saved tries to follow the Godliness that is outside of him and tries to resist the evil that is within him. However, since sin *is* within him and God is outside him, the sinner will continue to sin until he asks for and receives the Holy Ghost which cleanses him from all filth, sin, and evil. The evil spirit is then placed *outside* of him and forbidden to enter into him anymore.

However, Christians believe that even though they continue to hold onto the evil spirit which causes them to sin, God is also going to place His Holy Spirit with them *and* the evil spirit. This cannot be done because God does not dwell with evil and none shall enter into his kingdom. Remember, Jesus said the Kingdom of God is *within* you!

As I said, Christians believe that *after* they die they are changed to be holy. How can God give the Holy Ghost to a person *after* he dies when after he is dead, he can no longer choose to accept or reject anything? One cannot deny himself *after* he is dead because his *mortal* self is gone! Indeed, if he dies in his sin, he has denied God. His last decision is his final one.

That is why God gives the Holy Ghost, so that one is kept free from evil at all times, *especially* in one's last moments. Otherwise, when one's time to depart this world arrives, Satan will make known to that person that the person belongs to Satan by showing him the sin to which he still holds! Satan has told him the *truth* and it is undeniable! However, the holy person just tells him he's a liar and the Holy Ghost prevents Satan from stealing the soul in which He dwells. The Holy Ghost shows the undeniable truth of this to all and the holy person doesn't just *believe* it, he *knows* it! He continuously *experiences* it within him. That isn't even an, I dwell with you, with the Holy Spirit going in an out of you as He does *before* you get filled with the Holy Ghost.

If one is not holy when he passes, he has died in his sin and God is not going to allow him a place in the resurrection of the holy. Furthermore, it is well known that in the resurrection of the holy children of God, they are separated from all evil and are lifted up to dwell with Jesus Christ, leaving behind all evil, never to run together anymore. Therefore, how could the Holy Ghost reprove the world of sin, as Jesus said the Holy Ghost would do, if one has to wait to be resurrected to receive him? The world could *not* be reproved because the holy children of God are no longer in the world. And if so called holy people are *still* sinners, then how could the Holy Ghost reprove the world of sin when he can't even prevent it in the one He dwells in? *That* is why Christians are truly mocked, because they *know* this Christian claim of being holy and yet still a sinner is crap! Clearly one must receive the Holy Ghost in this mortal lifetime as Peter told Cornelius, the first Gentile to receive the Holy Ghost,

> 33 Immediately therefore I sent to thee; and thou hast well done that thou art come. Now therefore are we all here present before God, to hear all things that are commanded thee of God.
> 34 Then Peter opened his mouth, and said, Of a truth I perceive that God is no respecter of persons;
> 35 But in every nation he that feareth him, and worketh righteousness, is accepted by him.
> 36 The word which God sent unto the children of Israel, preaching peace by Jesus Christ: (he is Lord of all:)
> 37 That word, I say, ye know, which was published throughout all Judea, and began from Galilee, after the baptism that John preached;
> 38 How God anointed Jesus of Nazareth with the Holy Ghost and with power: who went about doing good, and healing all that were oppressed of the devil; for God was with him.
> 39 And we are witnesses of all things which he did both in the land of the Jews, and in Jerusalem; whom they slew and hanged on a tree:

40 Him God raised up the third day, and shewed him openly;

41 Not to all the people, but unto witnesses chosen before of God, even to us, who did eat and drink with him after he rose from the dead.

42 And he commanded us to preach unto the people, and to testify that it is he which was ordained of God to be the Judge of quick and dead.

43 To him give all the prophets witness, that through his name whosoever believeth in him shall receive remission of sins.

44 While Peter yet spake these words, the Holy Ghost fell on all them that heard the word.

45 And they of the circumcision which believed were astonished, as many as came with Peter, because that on the Gentiles also was poured out the gift of the Holy Ghost. (Acts chapter 10)

The mind, heart, and soul of those who truly seek righteousness have only one continuous prayer, that is that they do *only* righteousness, or, in other words, to cease from sinning. Cornelius and his friends and family, having that longing and that much sense, and believing on Jesus Christ, when they heard that whosoever believeth in Him shall receive remission of sins, believed with all their hearts that they would be made so that they would no longer sin in this world, otherwise remission of sins is *not* remission at all. But more than that, they *knew* that God desired it, for to goodness this makes *perfect* sense. They knew that as long as one sins, he is not free from the devil. They sought to be free from sin by not sinning anymore and they understood that Jesus Christ came to free people from the devil's oppression. They believed and they received. What you *don't* believe, you *cannot* receive, Christians! Then it isn't real to you!

~ FAITH, GRACE, WORKS, AND RELIGIOUS CONFUSION ~

Clearly, one must receive the Holy Ghost in this lifetime. Clearly, Christians worship in vain a god that does *not* exist because the Holy Ghost, which is One with and part of Almighty God, is not real to them, nor can He be found in them. Christians are like the pagans that had faith in their stone idols which were no gods nor represented any real God. Out of the Christians stoney heart they have constructed a false god through their religious doctrine, even as the Pharisees set up their idols in their hearts. Jesus spoke about this,

> 6 ... This people honoureth me with their lips, but their heart is far from me.
> 7 Howbeit in vain do they worship me, teaching for doctrine the commandments of men ...
> 8 For laying aside the commandment of God, ye hold the traditions of men ...
> 9 ... Full well ye reject the commandment of God, that ye may keep your own tradition.
> (Mark chapter 7)

That which hath been is now.

If Christians are looking for forgiveness, they had better look for it while they are still here and *not* be halfhearted about it. If they wait to go to the grave to fully ask for God's forgiveness, they waited too long. God's forgiveness *is* the Holy Ghost! For when one receives the Holy Ghost, *that* is when one's debt is canceled and he is restored to the condition of one who is truly free. That is what it is to be forgiven. If a vagabond is brought in chains to the King and the King forgives him but removes not his chains, clearly that forgiveness wasn't real! For God, a sinner who truly repents, is freed from the chains of sin by making him holy, pure, with all evil nature *removed*, with a new heart, new spirit, made *perfect!* Otherwise, before *God,* the truly repentant person is still in chains.

The sinner owes a debt of punishment and deserves condemnation. That is why Adam was driven out of the Garden of Eden. He was no longer allowed to partake of the Tree of Life, to live forever, neither did he nor does anyone *deserve* forgiveness. Forgiveness is not deserved, but is only by the grace of God. Yet, it pleases God to forgive those who are truly repentant and to return to them that which man drove away by their trespasses against God. The returning to man of the tree of eternal life, which is the Holy Ghost, reestablishes man into God's eternally good grace and therefore is God's true forgiveness.

By that, God is saying, I do not any longer hold my blessing away from you because I do not hold your sins against you, and I allow you once again the privilege of eternal life. This is surely the grace of God. Yet, even more grace than just returning eternal life to man, because Jesus Christ suffered to *increase* the power of the Holy Ghost within *mortality* by Him going through and overcoming all temptations and the suffering of death, so that His Holy Ghost should be a keeper and protector for man against all evil, thus ensuring the holy person eternal life. You see, every time Jesus was tempted, had pains, and even suffering death, He built up *new* strength and understanding within mortality that had not existed before. Therefore, with the power of the Holy Ghost, one has all power over Satan. So how then do Christians claim Satan still has power over them by beguiling them to continue to sin?

True faith is based on the understanding of God and his ways and waiting for the promises that are the results of God's inherent loving ways. With this knowledge and faith one does not wait on Him in vain and one orders all of his searching, thoughts, and feelings to first

FAITH, GRACE, WORKS, AND RELIGIOUS CONFUSION

receive the Holy Ghost, God's forgiveness, and then to hold on to the Holy Ghost even in the face of being killed. Many will tell such a one that no one can be perfect in this lifetime, but, because of his faith and knowledge of God, he knows that when one receives the Holy Ghost, he is perfect from that time on, having been born anew of God. Not only that, but the holy person *experiences* perfection continuously. I will tell you, the unimpeded and continuously growing life, love, truth, understanding, wisdom, justice, peace, and faith is amazing! Like a tree that adds more branches and roots, so do holy people continuously grow in goodness. That ain't from Bible study or monotonous prayers, dear Christians.

However, I explain about this birth in relation to perfection. Just like a child grows to be an adult, one also grows in the Holy Ghost to reach an ever unfolding state of perfection which, for lack of better words, is more perfect than the previous time. For example, God made people to be born as infants and this design is perfect because all God's designs are perfect to the purpose unto which He makes them. Yet, God's will is not for the infant to stay an infant but to grow to adulthood where more and more knowledge and abilities enfold him. So also is one who is filled with the Holy Ghost made perfect, being once again born an infant but not an infant in flesh, but of the Spirit of God.

A babe in Christ. The Holy Ghost filled person is perfect because he will no longer do evil, nor will his heart, because all evil and sin have been casted out of him. Yet, he grows deeper and deeper in God's love and understanding as the Holy Ghost nurtures and raises him. This growth in goodness squeezes out the remnants of old patterns like a tree sheds its outer bark as the growth rings push ever outward. Because God is infinite, there are always higher heights and deeper depths in Him into which His children are raised. Unfortunately, Christians have a very oversimplified, Satan encouraged, view of perfection. To Christians, perfection is *only* the ultimate in perfection which is God. But that leaves absolutely no room for God to create *anything* perfect, according to Christians' definition. *Fools!* So it is impossible for God to create something perfect? So He must always only create *corruption?* Do my readers see now what I meant earlier by the Christians can't think, can't reason, and have their poor little minds trapped in a Scriptural box with a hamster wheel inside, each rung being made out of a mere quote from Scripture? They are also unaware that even God *grows* for eternity! Well, of course! He is Life!

Thus God's children achieve an ever greater state of perfection. Even after the resurrection, that will always be true. Being perfect does not mean being God. Being perfect means not going against God's will, not sinning. But it *also* means *unity* with God, being one with Him. As Jesus said, That they may be one, Father, as we are one, thou in me and I in thee, and I in them and they in me. Since Love is forever growing, so also do the perfect holy children of God forever grow in God's perfect Love.

The faith which comes from the understanding of God opens the door for one to do certain works which without such faith he cannot do. Those works are the opening of one's self to the Holy Ghost, the complete denying of one's self, and forsaking everything for Jesus Christ, and, also, the suffering of the onslaught of evil which will try to destroy one's faith, soul, and body.

True faith instantly translates into those works and many other actions based on the understanding of that faith so that even faith itself can be seen as a work! Faith *is* work because it accepts, confirms,

～ FAITH, GRACE, WORKS, AND RELIGIOUS CONFUSION ～

and gives proper actions, such as the ones just named, but also the trusting of the Holy Ghost once it is received. It is the knowledge contained in that faith which allows acceptance of all the newness being born again creates, newness that takes some getting used to!

When a carpenter pounds in a nail, it is with both the eye to see and guide, and the hand, arm, and shoulder to pound. The work of the eye is considered a part of the whole work of pounding in the nail. Faith is the eye and guidance to accept and do whatsoever the Spirit of God would have one to do. Hence, Saint Paul recounts the prophets, saying, The just shall live by faith. Why? Because faith is the work of the heart and soul which brings forth the embracing and fulfilling of all other works of obedience to God which are recorded in the Law, the Prophets, and the Gospels of Jesus Christ. As Jesus answered the people when they asked,

> 28 ... What shall we do that we might work the works of God?
> 29 Jesus answered and said unto them, This is the work of God, that ye believe on him whom he hath sent. (John chapter 6)

The works of God are only accessible through the door of true faith and that faith is a part of every work which it embraces, As Jesus also testifies,

> Verily, verily I say unto you, He that believeth on me, the work that I do shall he do also; and greater works than these shall he do; because I go unto my Father. (John chapter 14 vs 12)

To this oneness of faith and works, James gives testimony,

> 13 For he shall have judgment without mercy, that hath shewed no mercy; and mercy rejoiceth against judgment.

14 What does it profit, my brethren, though a man say he hath faith, and have not works? Can faith save him?

15 If a brother or sister be naked, and destitute of daily food,

16 And one of you say unto them, Depart in peace, be ye warmed and filled; notwithstanding ye give them not those things which are needful to the body; what does it profit?

17 Even so faith, if it hath not works, is dead, being alone.

18 Yea, a man may say, Thou hast faith, and I have works: shew me thy faith without thy works, and I will shew thee my faith by my works.

19 Thou believeth that there is one God; thou doest well: the devils also believe and tremble.

20 But wilt thou know, O vain man, that faith without works is dead?

21 Was not Abraham our father justified by works, when he had offered Isaac his son upon the altar?

22 Seest thou how faith wrought with his works, and by works was faith made perfect?

23 And the scripture was fulfilled which saith, Abraham believed God, and it was imputed unto him for righteousness: and he was called the Friend of God.

24 Ye see then how that by works a man is justified, and not by faith only.

25 Likewise also was not Rahab the harlot justified by works, when she had received the messengers, and had sent them out another way?

26 For as the body without the spirit is dead, so faith without works is dead also. (James chapter 2)

~ FAITH, GRACE, WORKS, AND RELIGIOUS CONFUSION ~

The works that James is speaking about are those works which are born from the instant translation of true faith into the inspired action. These are aptly called, works of faith. I say, true faith, because it is guided by the Spirit of God which always guides one into true works of faith, However, James is speaking about two kinds of faith. The faith that is without works, he calls dead faith. My question then is, If it is dead faith, then what kind of faith is it, and is it really faith at all? James explains what it is by making mention that the devils also believe and tremble. That kind of dead faith is no more than the acknowledgment of the reality of God. The devils are forced to believe because God is the power that casts them out and they cannot resist. The devils' belief is established as a consequence of fact, the fact that Almighty God is real, and, they've known so from the very beginning, having dwelled in the beginning into the Kingdom of God in Heaven. Yet, their belief in God, indeed, their absolute certainty that God is real, is of no profit to them but to assure them that they will soon be judged and eternally tormented.

The devils' faith in God is not profitable because they despise the works of God. They despise the works of God because His works are Love, Peace, Truth, Justice, perfect and Holy. However, the devils want to do things their own way. Self without the leading of the goodness and love of God is only evil. Why? Because where there is no goodness, there is evil, for that is what evil is, a consciousness without any goodness, or, in other words, a conscious existing death! Everything brought forth from that dark consciousness must be contrary to the Good God.

The demons' condition exists in much the same way Christians have unprofitable faith. Their conscience is forced to accept the reality of Jesus Christ because they know He is real and to not believe is damnation. However, though they believe Jesus to be the Son of God, they kill their faith by subordinating it to their empty selves. What ever their works may be, these seem good to the empty self of them, so that is what they do. *That* is why every Sunday morning their sermons are so boring, like a freshman college lecture, like a conscious existing death! They went to man's *school* to learn how to preach for Almighty God. So sad!

However, to allow themselves to be filled with the Holy Ghost or even to be led to get filled with the Holy Ghost, that is not pleasing to them because then their faith and works would be true and alive, albeit *without* man's imposed structure. But man's imposed structure is what comforts them, not the true faith in Jesus where their works would be of the Holy Ghost and not of themselves.

All Christians have is just a belief. They do not want true faith which brings about and is a part of true works of God. True faith is more than just a belief in God. True faith is the work of the heart and soul which accepts the Spirit of God to continually guide a person. True faith yields continuous perfection! How could it not because true faith only happens when you have completely given all to the will of God, *thy* will be done in me.

Yet, Christians suborn their conscience into believing they are the chosen children of God merely because they believe He is real. The Pharisees did the same except that they were *born* into the people chosen by God. If *they* couldn't be justified for ignoring the Spirit of God, surely neither can Christians be justified. Christians are to Jesus Christ even as the Pharisees were to GOD the Father, because neither accepts the Spirit of Truth that was sent to them, yet, both call God's name often. Please do not confuse the holy children of God to be Christians. Peter and Paul and all of Christ's

FAITH, GRACE, WORKS, AND RELIGIOUS CONFUSION

true followers were holy because they were filled with the Holy Ghost of Jesus Christ.

I have often explained to Christians that they must forsake everything for Jesus Christ, even down to their own will, and that then the Holy Spirit will always be with them and guide them into all truth. Their response is always, But to be perfect is impossible because then we wouldn't be human any more. Surely their words testify against themselves. First, because they doubt the power and Holy Spirit of God, second, because they don't want to forsake what they call being human. Their saying, even lamenting that, 'Then we wouldn't be human anymore,' testifies that they love their self as they know it more than what God could make them to be. They love their own ways more than God's ways and do not want to completely deny themselves for Jesus Christ.

The ways in which God makes a holy person are unfailing because they are born of the Holy Ghost, the third part of the triune God, as Christians like to describe it. They *say* all parts of the triune are equal but they sure as Hell don't act that way, nor have any other supporting beliefs that *must* exist in them if they had true faith in a *triune* God!

The ways in which a person *makes himself* will always fail because the self is born of something separated from God and therefore easily tends toward evil, having rejected the ways of God in order to have *self*-authority. This turning more evil is not necessarily apparent to people because many will say that they know a lot of good people who aren't even Christians. OK! And many branches cut from a tree look just fine, look alive for a while. . . until they don't. And in a dim light, the withering is harder to detect. On the other hand, though, there is nothing inherently failing about being a human being, just as there is nothing inherently failing about being an angel. One third of the angels failed God but two-thirds did not. Likewise, there are those human beings who will not fail God and there are those who will fail Him. In a previously published book, God's Creative Writing, why and how they all failed at some point is deeply explained, including *why* God's plan for Creation allotted for such failure! One might wonder why such a book was published *before* this one, as usually the more basic understandings come first. True. But this book was written thirty years ago and the manuscript sat on my shelf till some dear folks read it and demanded I publish it, too!

Yet, in order for Christians to keep their pre-eminence to themselves and others, they claim God is going to save them after they die in their wicked condition, and they *know* they are a failure. However, they won't fully give themselves up to Christ, and even in the face of death many of them will still hold to their religion and reject the Holy Ghost. Just like the Pharisees. That which hath been is now. Only *if* the Christians hold Jesus to be more important than their religion do they have a chance when they are passing away to receive the Holy Ghost! It might make sense to them *then*, finally, that they can give their *whole* life up to Jesus, because they are dying! Something like when Jesus redeemed the thief on the cross! He stole worldly goods, the Christians stole spiritual goods! Neither had enough concern for the owner. But one thief truly repented while dying. . . what about the other? What about *you* dear Christians?

The reason why there is no forgiveness for blaspheming against the Holy Ghost is because once a person is made perfect by the Holy Ghost, given a new heart, a new spirit, there is nothing that can compel or trick that person to sin. Before being filled with the Holy Ghost, the evil spirit within that person can force him to sin either through sheer pressure or devious manipulations. Yet, seeking Jesus Christ with all ones

~ FAITH, GRACE, WORKS, AND RELIGIOUS CONFUSION ~

heart, soul, mind, and strength cuts Satan down considerably until you are able to cut him down *completely* to do *one* thing- truly repent and receive the Holy Ghost! Anyone who is *truly* sincere toward their love for the Lord Jesus Christ, this true repentance is *exactly, undauntingly* what they will seek until their prayers are answered. And they *will* be.

In order for a Holy Ghost filled person to sin, he has to decide to reject God's ways as Lucifer freely did in the beginning. That is why there is no forgiveness for blaspheming against the Holy Ghost because it is a noncompelled decision to reject the Love, Truth, Peace, and Life of God. Adam and Eve were tricked to disobey God and that is why man has a second chance at eternal life. Man died because he disobeyed God, but because he was tricked and remorseful for his sin, God made forgiveness accessible to him.

However, Lucifer had no regrets, neither did anyone trick him to disobey God. He tricked himself and then decided to justify it. In fact, his whole existence since then has been, to himself, one giant justification, feeling that the more evil he is, the *more* he is justified in saying, Look *God,* you see how far removed I am from *you?* See how free I am? I *don't* have to be like *you* just serving *your* glory, being a slave to you. And I'll show everyone else the *real* truth! Well, Satan does show *his* 'truth' about evil but from *his* perspective. All of this is why there is no forgiveness for Satan, because when God showed him he was wrong, from God's perspective, Satan eternally hardened his own heart. The Spirit of God says to Christians and to all people, Harden not your hearts because you cannot receive forgiveness while opposing the Living God. Being a slave to perfect goodness is the freest anyone can ever be, as free as the Lord Jesus Christ is because we live *inside* Him and He *in* us. All ya gotta do is believe Jesus can make you perfect right here in mortality then seek Him till He shows you how to *truly* repent and receive the Holy Ghost. No matter how long that takes. No matter what. No matter how long you walk in the *unknown* with *known* true faith! I strongly recommend The Faithwalker Series by Darryl Markowitz if you want *a lot* of deep examples of this. I call the fiction series Fantasy that is real!

I now want to present two of Paul's discussions on faith in which he describes how faith, and not works, justifies a person. Paul also uses Abraham, as James did, as an example to convey the necessary understanding of faith. James and Paul seem to reach opposing conclusions in which James shows that justification comes from works and Paul demonstrates justification comes from faith. However, they do *not* oppose one another and I shall discuss this after presenting the following Scriptures:

2 This only would I learn from you, Received ye the Spirit by the works of the law, or by the hearing of faith?

3 Are ye so foolish? Having begun in the Spirit, are ye now made perfect by the flesh?

4 Have ye suffered so many things in vain? If it be yet in vain.

5 He therefore that ministereth to you the Spirit, and worketh miracles among you, doeth he it by the works of the law, or by the hearing of faith?

6 Even as Abraham believed God, and it was accounted to him for righteousness.

7 know ye therefore that they which are of faith, the same are the children of Abraham.

8 And the Scripture, foreseeing that God would justify the heathen through faith, preached before the gospel unto Abraham, saying, In thee shall all nations be blessed.

FAITH, GRACE, WORKS, AND RELIGIOUS CONFUSION

9 So then they which be of faith are blessed with faithful Abraham.

10 For as many as are of the works of the law are under the curse: for it is written, Cursed is everyone that continueth not in all things which are written in the book of the law to do them.

11 But that no man is justified by the law in the sight of God, it is evident: for, The just shall live by faith.

12 And the law is not of faith: but, The man that doeth them shall live in them.

(Galatians Chapter 3)

What shall we say then that Abraham our father, as pertaining to the flesh, hath found?

2 For if Abraham were justified by works, he hath whereof to glory; but not before God.

3 For what sayeth the scripture? Abraham believed God, and it was counted unto him for righteousness.

4 Now to him that worketh is the reward not reckoned of grace, but of debt.

5 But to him that worketh not, but believeth on him that justifieth the ungodly, his faith is counted for righteousness.

6 Even as David also describeth the blessedness of the man, unto whom God imputeth righteousness without works,

7 Saying, Blessed are they whose iniquities are forgiven, and whose sins are covered.

8 Blessed is the man to whom the Lord will not impute sin. . .

13 For the promise, that he should be the heir of the world, was not to Abraham, or to his seed, through the law, but through the righteousness of faith. . .

16 Therefore it is of faith, that it might be of grace; to the end the promise might be sure to all the seed; not to that only which is of the law, but to that also which is of the faith of Abraham; who is the father of us all,

17 (As it is written, I have made thee a father of many nations,) before him whom he believed, even God, who quickeneth the dead, and calleth those things which be not as though they were.

18 Who against hope believed in hope, that he might become the father of many nations, according to that which was spoken, So shall thy seed be.

19 And being not weak in faith, he considered not his own body now dead, when he was about an hundred years old, neither yet the deadness of Sarah's womb:

20 He staggered not at the promise of God through unbelief; but was strong in faith, giving glory to God;

21 And being fully persuaded that, what he had promised, he was able to perform.

22 And therefore it was imputed to him for righteousness.

23 Now it was not written for his sake alone, that it was imputed to him;

24 But for us also, to whom it shall be imputed, if we believe on him that raised up Jesus our Lord from the dead;

25 Who was delivered for our offenses, and was raised again for our justification. (Romans Chapter 4)

I must first comment on verses 5-8 of Romans because it is verses like these that religious people use to try to justify their false doctrine of claiming to be children of God and yet still sinning. However, a

∽ FAITH, GRACE, WORKS, AND RELIGIOUS CONFUSION ∽

sinner receives justification not to continue to sin, but, having sinned in the past, he is given forgiveness so that sin should be discontinued and righteousness resumed. A debt is not forgiven in order for another to be accrued. It is not ungodliness that God justifies, but the person turning *away* from evil and thus being raised alive from the deadness of his sinful condition. He receives forgiveness, which *is* justification, because the sinner turns toward truth and goodness which God is justifying and *not* ungodliness. The sinner begs for God's mercy, which, if he doesn't squander, he is justified by proving his heart is sincere to love God. This is what Paul is saying when speaking about justifying the ungodly. God justifies those who are sincerely repentant.

Now, the sinner had not done works that brought forth riches, but sin that brought forth debt. Therefore, Paul says that to him that works not, his *faith* is counted for righteousness, and, whom God imputeth righteousness without works, and, Blessed is the man to whom the Lord will not impute sin. *Past* sin, not sin *after* one is forgiven because forgiveness is a trust, which, if broken, it is lost. Implied in the asking of forgiveness is the promise to yield unto the Master to do only His will and to not return to defying Him. Therefore sin is not imputed to those who are forgiven, that they may have a chance to make good on their promise to God. God then entrusts to them the riches that Adam squandered, the eternal Holy Spirit, which now being the Holy Ghost, ensures one's keeping of the promise. The Law of God could not ensure this because to keep the law depended on man's will to keep it, which is too weak. Yet, the potential to be preserved by the law existed. But *what kind* of preservation?

The last verse I quoted from Galatians, And the law is not of faith: but, The man that doeth them shall live in them; this indicates that if one completes all the appropriate actions then he shall live in the riches of the righteousness in his actions. However, to me it seems that to believe this also requires faith, as evidenced by many people's lack of faith in not recognizing the inherent reward of righteous actions and not seeing a benefit of life in them. However, those degenerate people neither Paul nor even the religious regard and his words are not addressed to them. But again, what *kind* of benefit is inherent in keeping the Law?

Paul says the law is not of faith because the rewards for doing something tangible (keeping the Law) are not expected or received through faith but are the result of the direct consequence of the action, as is the reward of the inherent righteousness in keeping God's law. However, it is obvious that God owes nothing to man, no matter what man does, and that man owes everything to God, no matter what man does. Paul points out that man's reward must result from faith and not works, since God is indebted to no one, and work implies the owing of a debt (Romans verses 2-5) Thus, Paul says that Abraham is not justified before God by works (Romans verse 2)

So much ignorance and lack of seeking Understanding. The inherent righteousness in *doing* the Law of God truly has a certain life within it, as described by the list of blessings Moses recited if you keep all the Law. *Besides* the fact that *only* Jesus kept *all* the law, take a look at those listed blessings! They are all for *here* in mortal life. There was *no* power within keeping the Law of God that allowed *mortal* life to continue on forever! Even Jesus died a *mortal* death in following His Father's command. Once Adam gave eternal mortality up, that was a done deal never to return! God doesn't *owe* us *that* anymore because there is *no* work we can do that He *should* owe us *that*!

But the *promise* is that in keeping all righteousness of the Law then ye shall live, in that you escape the *judgment* of a sinner for you having lived mortally righteous. But *that* one promise extends to

~ FAITH, GRACE, WORKS, AND RELIGIOUS CONFUSION ~

immortality. But *how*? Because contained within the Law of God is the command that *all* mankind would be required to hearken unto the Messiah, which *is* the Lord Jesus Christ who commanded us to be born again! However, the command to follow Messiah is part of the *Law of God* so therefore cannot preserve eternal *mortality* either! But only through the fulfilling of the command to follow Jesus the Messiah can our *souls* live eternally. *This* distinction was ever present in Paul's mind when he multiplied all his words trying to describe this clearly! So he divides all the Law of God away from that one command to follow Jesus. That last command requires *perfect* faith to be fulfilled while all the others he considers to be mere works because the actions of obedience are so *simply* taught.

This is also one of the reasons why Paul said that by the *deeds* of the law there shall no flesh be justified in God's sight, for who can stand before God and tell Him that he did a great deed that deserves *eternal life*? Also, obeying God and keeping all of God's law is *required* and *expected* of man because that preserves for the man the free gift of life that God supplies to him. So then, it is no great deed to preserve a gift, but it is *expected*. No thanks are due to the person who preserves the gift, but all thanks are due to the One who gives it. The great deed is in the giving of the gift. Shame to those who squander it. Knowing man's failure and weakness and that God is the Creator, one should realize that it is only by God's grace that a man is forgiven and justified unto eternal life and that man's deeds are not sufficient, just like Abraham with Sarah, being way past ability to have children, believed and received through their faith the grace of a new life by Isaac's conception! It is the Archetype of receiving the Holy Ghost!

There was no specific, tangible *action* that Abraham and Sarah did in order to receive the blessing of having their child Isaac in their extreme old age when their natural ability had long since passed from them. All they had at that time was a promise from God, in which if they hadn't faithfully believed, it would not have been fulfilled. The receiving of a reward from none other than believing in the words God spoke to them is called faith by Paul. Had they not had this faith, then the Messiah, who was promised to ensure an eternal life in an eternal kingdom of peace, couldn't have been born. In this way, Paul says, The just shall live by faith, because the receiving of everyone's ultimate goal (eternal life) is not fulfilled by tangible works with understandable, predictable consequences, but the goal is fulfilled by the unseen action of faith. Such faith all people should have to the receiving of the Holy Ghost and perfection here on Earth. However, I point out that Abraham's faith continuously guided him to do all obedience to God, which if he hadn't have fulfilled would have shown in him some *lack* of love for God and stifled his faith. As God said, For I know him, that he shall command his house after him, and they shall keep the way of the Lord. In other words, God knew Abraham's *faith* would produce certain *works!*

Faith in God rests on love for God. If one does not have perfect love for God then his faith slips through the cracks because true faith is the belief that God will save those who whole-heartedly and sincerely come to him. The proper definition of love is that state of consciousness which *fully* embraces unto goodness that which is loved. Anything short of such whole-heartedness may be called *like* but *not* truly love. *Like* is, Yea, that's OK but push comes to shove I can do without it. *Love* places what is loved in the number one slot of their priorities. This is why the two great commandments are what they are. Love the Lord God with *all* your heart, soul, mind, and strength. Love your neighbor as yourself. And if all you can do is *like* yourself,

~ FAITH, GRACE, WORKS, AND RELIGIOUS CONFUSION ~

well, obviously you have a problem you really need to fix! Sooner than later would be wise.

Faith is the cornerstone of salvation because faith leads one to *do* things that are wise before God, yet, often foolish to the world. In ignoring the foolish, common opinion of the world and even one's own five senses to follow the leading of the Holy Spirit of God one further establishes that his love and faith is true and real. He did not doubt it. However, if one were to ignore what his faith is leading him to do then he does not do the work of faith so his faith is disannulled in doubt and lack of appreciation. His faith would not bear the test of the work that faith requires.

If Abraham had not offered up his son Isaac when he was commanded to do so, then Abraham would have doubted his knowledge of God being all good and he would not be faithful nor love God with all his heart. However, by obeying the faith he had in God, he hearkened to what he believed was God's commandment, knowing that only good would come from God. No harm would come to Isaac. Wherefore, doubting nothing about God, Abraham told his servants before he went to sacrifice his son, Wait here until I and the lad come again to you.

Thus, when Abraham was tested by being sent to sacrifice his son Isaac, Abraham did not slacken his love for God even to favor his dearly precious and most favored son, and God replied, Hurt not the lad for now I know that thou fearest God. Evil wanted Abraham to doubt God or to love Isaac more than God, thus turning Abraham away from God. However, Abraham's faith overcame all that was trying to destroy him. One doesn't know how strong his faith is until it is tested.

Thus James said that by works was faith made perfect. However, these works are the works of faith and not of perceived tangible reward.

Therefore, Paul and James do not at all disagree. The works that Paul speaks about are those with perceived tangible consequences which are not of faith, being of the known law of God, but the works that James speaks about are the works of faith which prove, strengthen, justify, and come from ones faith. Those depend on the will of God to guide one into the unknown, yet, via a *seeing* faith! Not a *blind* faith. For God is Understanding and loathes blindness of any sort. Abraham's faith is a *seeing faith,* having an eye that sees, and a heart that hears, as opposed to how God chastised Israel through the prophets and Jesus, saying, Ye have eyes that see not, nor ears that hear, and a hardened heart that loves darkness and not light. What do holy people and truly sincere seeking people see with their faith? The true essence of reality! That God is *only* Good *always*. For they know God is seven Holy Spirits in One that all together cannot be moved. Life. Love. Truth. Peace. Understanding. Justice. Wisdom. I AM that I *AM*. Because all seven are mutually supportive of each other *eternally.* Thus being the *essence of BEING. Omniscient. Omnipotent. Omnipresent.* Take a moment and meditate on each of the seven and you will feel what they all have in common! I *AM*. Then imagine removing just one of the seven and see what the other six look like without it.

Faith is *not* justified by faith and neither is work justified by work, but, faith justifies work, and work justifies faith. A beautiful marriage, perfectly complementary. The reason why James speaks about works and Paul focuses on faith can be explained by the following example: Paul and James both shook hands. Paul said James shook his hand. James said Paul shook his hand. Such is faith and the works of faith. They cannot exist without being together. Thus James' two statements, Seest thou how faith wrought with his works, and by works was faith made perfect? And, Ye see then how that by works a man

FAITH, GRACE, WORKS, AND RELIGIOUS CONFUSION

is justified, and not by faith only. Not by works or faith alone but by both together.

Many religious leaders fear *too much faith*, frankly because they know crazy people will go off and do something crazy and call it a work of faith. You hear these stories often enough thrown up by mainstream media *knowing* the foolish Christian leaders will be kept in check by the fear these stories produce. Not *too much* faith *and* make sure you run *all* your faith through the Christian leaders. They will make sure the crazies are weeded out. Hmmm, tisk, tisk! So easily controlled by evil. That's what the religious did to Jesus! Called Him crazy. Now, there were plenty of crazy people back then and *worse*. Did Jesus let that diminish *anything* about what He is or was doing? Of course not. But for Christians it really gets tricky, doesn't it, when they feel they have to please the world, too!

To obey God's law is done by one's own will and people often expect a reward or direct consequence from that which they willfully do. In the case of willful obedience to God, one's reward is inherent in the righteousness of their actions because there is no guilt or death in them. Thus life is not taken or destroyed from them. However, because of man's weakness and the evil nature that was passed down to him ever since Adam disobeyed God, man is neither pure nor able to keep all of God's law. Therefore, because man cannot do anything tangible to ensure his life and bring himself into the necessary perfection to have eternal life, man must rely upon that which is not of his own will. Man must rely on the will of God which is only done in us through faith in God to have it done so. Hence again, The just shall live by faith. The giving up of one's own will to God, in order for God's will to be done in him, forfeits claim to any direct consequences gainable from one's own control, having ceded one's own will to God. This situation is indeed faith. One has faith in God through the receiving and keeping of the Holy Ghost that he will be led in his heart, soul, mind, and actions into all righteousness. He still has the ability of his free will to disobey God, for God returns his free will to him, but without anything being able to trick or compel him to disobey, he will remain faithful to his love for God, no matter what.

Because James was facing many people who believed, yet were *not* filled with the Holy Ghost (as the Holy Scripture says that many believers were added to them but did not join them. Acts chapter 5) he said, But wilt thou know O vain man, that faith without works is dead? I have already described that type of faith. It is merely a belief that God is real, or that Jesus really is the Son of God, However, it is not the true faith of understanding (or as Paul calls it, faith from hearing) but rather just a stagnant belief and therefore does not lead one to do the works of faith: denying oneself, picking up his cross, and getting filled with the Holy Ghost. So Christians faith is dead, like stagnant water that has fouled, because it does not bring forth the works of God, but only the works of themselves.

Watch people at any Christian service in *any* church. Watch them during church then *after* when they are leaving. Watch their faces, feel their spirits. When service is over it's like they turn off the Jesus switch. Don't worry, it'll be turned back on next Sunday for a short time. And all *this* is why Jesus shall say unto them in His coming, Depart from me, I never knew you.

Christians like to quote the Holy Scripture that faith comes from hearing. However, Christians think that hearing is mere sound, when, in fact, it is perceiving meaning, which means *understanding*. And how can they understand if there isn't some goodness in them which says, This makes sense. Which is the greater love dear Christians?

~ FAITH, GRACE, WORKS, AND RELIGIOUS CONFUSION ~

Merely giving you a new name to call God but you continue to sin, or, making you a new heart, a new spirit and giving it to you so you *won't* sin anymore? Which is true salvation? Alas, you Christians don't believe the most important part of the Holy Scripture, and so your doctrine makes absolutely no sense at all. And then you teach others to be feckless just like you. Shame on you! No wonder all your leaders have to come from your schools and *not* the Holy Ghost. Or do you really think the Holy Ghost must go to school *first* before you give Him *your* stamp of approval?

It is interesting to see that James faced people who were believers in Christ but not doers, as he told them, But be ye doers of the word, and not hearers only, deceiving your own selves (James chapter 1, verse 22). Having already heard and believed, what else could James say to these idle believers to exhort them into action? However, Paul faced many who purported themselves to be doers of God's law but they would not hear, out of unbelief, the *reasons* for the New Testament, but mainly the love of God the Father which sent Jesus Christ to offer a much better salvation. To those people, Paul stressed the importance of faith, whom, if they would have believed, most certainly would have been diligent to do the works of faith.

Because Paul and James were dealing with different peoples who were blind in different ways, *that* is why Paul spoke more of faith and James spoke more of works. Yet, clearly, if one examines Paul's life, his works of faith are numerous, having performed many miracles along with suffering much persecution for Christ's name.

23 . . . in labors more abundant, in stripes above measure, in prisons more frequent, in deaths oft.

24 Of the Jews five times received I forty stripes save one.

> 25 Thrice was I beaten with rods, once I was stoned, thrice I suffered ship wreck, a night and a day I have been in the deep;
> 26 In journeyings often, in perils of waters, in perils of robbers, in perils of mine own countrymen, in perils by the heathen, in perils in the city, in perils in the wilderness, in perils in the sea, in perils among false brethren;
> 27 In weariness and painfulness, in watchings often, in hunger and thirst, in fastings often, in cold and nakedness.
> 28 Beside those things that are without, that which cometh upon me daily, the care of all the churches. (2 Corinthians chapter 11)

All those things Paul suffered joyfully for the hope and faith that he had in Jesus Christ. Otherwise, without such faith Paul describes how one would be:

> 19 If in this life only we have hope in Christ, we are of all men most miserable ...
> 32 If after the manner of men I have fought with beasts at Ephesus, what advantageth it me, if the dead rise not? Let us eat and drink; for tomorrow we die.
> 33 Be not deceived: evil communications corrupt good manners (1 Corinthians chapter 15)

Paul did not count his life in this world to be dear to him, but for the glory of God unto eternal life he placed himself in constant danger for Christ's name sake.

Likewise, James, though he spoke much about works, culminated his life in the supreme act of faith in Jesus Christ.

> Now, about that time Herod the king stretched forth his hand to vex certain of the church.

~ FAITH, GRACE, WORKS, AND RELIGIOUS CONFUSION ~

2 And he killed James the brother of John with the sword. (Acts chapter 12)

From all this, one sees that though Paul spoke much about faith, he often verified his faith by deeds of faith. Though James spoke much about works, his deeds often testified of his faith. Both really were of the same mind, heart, faith, and deed, and, indeed were in full agreement.

Grace is the reward from God for the combination of one's faith and works of faith. Grace is the Holy Ghost. It cannot be earned, and it is not deserved, but, through faith and the works from that faith, God places the Holy Ghost within that soul, mind, heart, and body because God is very merciful. Faith is constantly being reassured by grace. Yet, faith constantly embraces grace by standing firm to do whatever works grace requires.

It is a shame to say, but because people do not have the knowledge of God, but claim to be of God, they have started many wars and slaughtered many people. They have blasphemed the Holy name of Jesus Christ. Catholics kill protestants. Protestants kill Catholics. And *both* have persecuted Jews by teachings and decrees taught to ignorant followers that Jews are devils and *should* be mistreated. But all different religions are contentious to one another. Jesus Christ is going to get rid of you all because you have drug his name through the mud. The Spirit of God says to you all, Change before it is too late and I will forgive you. Not much longer!

CHAPTER 4

FRUITS OF THE HOLY GHOST

6 Whosoever abideth in him sinneth not: whosoever sinneth hath not seen him, neither known him.
7 Little children, let no man deceive you: he that doeth righteousness is righteous, even as he is righteous.
8 He that committeth sin is of the devil; for the devil sinneth from the beginning. For this purpose the Son of God was manifested, that he might destroy the works of the devil.
9 Whosoever is born of God doth not commit sin; for his seed remaineth in him: and he cannot sin, because he is born of God. (1 John chapter 3)

5 Mortify therefore your members which are upon the Earth: fornication, uncleanness, inordinate affection, evil concupiscence, and covetousness, which is idolatry:
6 For which things sake the wrath of God cometh on the children of disobedience:
7 In the which ye also walked some time, when ye lived in them.

8 But now ye also put off all these; anger, wrath, malice, blasphemy, filthy communication out of your mouth.
9 Lie not to one another, seeing that ye have put off the old man with his deeds;
10 And have put on the new man, which is renewed in knowledge after the image of him that created him: (Colossians chapter 3)

18 We know that whosoever is born of God sinneth not; but he that is begotten of God keepeth himself, and that wicked one toucheth him not.
19 And we know that we are of God, and the whole world lieth in wickedness.
(1 John chapter 5)

25 But whoso looketh into the perfect law of liberty, and continueth therein, he being not a forgetful hearer, but a doer of the work, this man shall be blessed in his deed.
26 If any man among you seem to be religious, and bridleth not his tongue, but deceiveth his own heart, this man's religion is in vain.
27 Pure religion and undefiled before God and the Father is this, To visit the fatherless and widows in their affliction, and to keep himself unspotted from the world. (James chapter 1)

James perceived the zeal in which many people pursued after Jesus Christ to obey Him. The word, *religious,* accurately testifies to that zeal and means *exactly* that, to be diligent and thorough about one's task. However, James knew that for all this zeal, unless they continued to seek God until they received the Holy Ghost, their *zeal* to serve

God would not be perfected and would turn to be unprofitable even as did the zeal of the Pharisees. Take note that the word *zeal* describes a strong concentration of effort by the *old will.* For people who are filled with the Holy Ghost do *not* serve Jesus Christ with zeal! We serve with something far beyond zeal! We serve by *being* the pure goodness the Holy Ghost has made us to *be!* That involves a whole different set of emotions natural to the new heart and new spirit and new will that we have, and we rejoice deeply in it.

However, though understanding those differences between the religious and the holy, James sought to preserve the goodness that was there in the religious. For one thing, there were a whole lot more mere believers *in* Jesus than there were holy people *of* Jesus, but Wisdom would have as much goodness preserved as possible whether holy or just believers.

Therefore, James brought to them the statement that pure, active religion must be unspotted from the world. To achieve *that,* one must be truly diligent. To be truly diligent, or *religious,* about serving God, one must continue to seek God until he rejects *all* that is not God's will, but also accept whatever God has for him to do, to *be, continuously* maintaining God's will in oneness with Him. This is none other than denying one's self and everything else for Jesus Christ, picking up his cross, and getting filled with the Holy Ghost. In other words, this is James best attempt at converting the zeal of the religious into something better!

Peter also stated quite clearly the way in which the children of God must be,

> 14 As obedient children, not fashioning yourselves according to the former lusts in your ignorance:

15 But as he which hath called you is holy, so be ye holy in all manner of conversation;

16 Because it is written, Be ye holy, for I the Lord am holy. (Peter chapter 1)

11 Finally, brethren, farewell. Be perfect, be of good comfort, be of one mind, live in peace; and the God of love and peace shall be with you.

12 Greet one another with an holy kiss.

13 All the saints salute you.

14 The grace of our Lord Jesus Christ, and the love of God, and the communion of the Holy Ghost, be with you all. AMEN. (Paul's words from 2 Corinthians chapter 12)

Jesus said,

Be ye therefore perfect, even as your Father which is in heaven is perfect.
(Matthew chapter 5, verse 48)

It could suffice to end the chapter here, my readers having now read about perfection from Peter, James, John, and Paul. However, since I have made many statements which to most people probably seem abundantly peculiar, I shall yet delve a bit deeper in the Scriptures to prove to my readers that in all my statements and conclusions there is no fabrication, but that they are in agreement with the Holy Scriptures.

Jesus said that the Holy Ghost would teach one of all things and lead one into all truth. After John received the Holy Ghost, he also testified that this is indeed what happens.

20 But ye have an unction from the Holy One, and ye know all things.
21 I have not written unto you because ye know not the truth, but because ye know it, and that no lie is of the truth. . .
27 But the anointing which ye have received of him abideth in you, and ye need not that any man teach you: but as the same anointing teacheth you all things, and is truth, and is no lie, and even as it hath taught you, ye shall abide in him.
28 And now, little children, abide in him; that, when he shall appear, we may have confidence, and not be ashamed before him at his coming. (1 John chapter 2)

Paul's writings also fulfill these words that Jesus spoke, That which is born of the flesh is flesh and that which is born of the Spirit is spirit.

4 That the righteousness of the law should be fulfilled in us, who walk not after the flesh, but after the Spirit.
5 For they that are after the flesh do mind the things of the flesh; but they that are after the Spirit the things of the Spirit.
6 For to be carnally minded is death; but to be spiritually minded is life and peace.
7 Because the carnal mind is enmity against God; for it is not subject to the law of God, neither indeed can be.
8 So then they that are in the flesh cannot please God.
9 But ye are not in the flesh, but in the Spirit, if so be that the Spirit of God dwell in you. Now if any man have not the Spirit of Christ, he is none of his. (Romans chapter 8)

These words Paul wrote to people who obviously were still dwelling on Earth. That meant they still had flesh bodies. Why then does Paul say in verse 9, But ye are not in the flesh. Paul is saying that though the children of God on Earth are in the flesh, they are not *of* the flesh because they do not walk after the flesh but after the Spirit. The person in the body is of the Holy Spirit of God and that person dwells in that Holy Spirit which in turn dwells within that flesh body. However, the person of the ungodly walks after the flesh, being mastered by the lusts thereof in which the evil spirit dwells.

To the world, a child of God and a child of the devil seem the same because they cannot see the Holy Spirit that insulates the child of God from being mastered by dumb flesh. Yet, in the following Scripture, Paul describes even more deeply how the Holy Ghost keeps a person who, though in the flesh, is not *of* the flesh. He spoke the following words to those who thought Paul was ungodly, walking after the flesh. Paul therefore describes in detail how the Holy Ghost intercedes in the children of God so that even all their thoughts are guided from their very origin into obedience to Jesus Christ. It has to be *all* of their thoughts from their very origin because Paul says *every* thought. Therefore, there is no room for even the beginning thoughts of evil. This is done for the children of God because they asked and continuously ask to so do. Coming up is Paul's description of the power and inner workings of the Holy Ghost within the children of God and how the Spirit fights their battles for them. For those who continuously seek to do righteousness, the battle is a constant one.

This continuous battle leads Paul to use the word *war,* instead of *walk* in the following Scripture. Paul says, we do not *war* after the flesh, because the children of God do not rely on self-righteousness, which comes from one's own fleshly self-will, but giving their will over to Jesus Christ through faith, their weapons of warfare are the Holy Ghost to which they continuously yield.

FRUITS OF THE HOLY GHOST

Before I record the Scripture below, I want to add some more depth to the previous paragraph. As I mentioned earlier, the manuscript for this book was written by me thirty years ago. Since then, the *tree* that Jesus had made me to *be* has grown considerably more branches and roots, which means branches of understanding of my mind and emotional understanding in the spreading roots of my heart. Only together, with mind and heart in unity, can a person perceive the Holy Spirit of God, for God is *One,* so inside us, we have to be *one* also, mind and heart in one, to be within the Oneness of Jesus.

I wrote two paragraphs ago that our weapons of warfare are the Holy Ghost. Now some might think I made a grammatical error and should have said, *weapon* of warfare *is* the Holy Ghost. No! For the Father, the Son, *and* the Holy Ghost have within them *seven* Holy Spirits of God. Seven in one like a seven-sided gem, each facet unique. Life, Love, Truth, Justice, Understanding, Wisdom, and Peace. Why do I mention this again? Imagine the kind of warfare wielded within holy people by *those* seven constantly confronting evil as it seeks to overcome us! Life is generative. Love is fully embracing of goodness and the strongest motivation. Truth *is* the sense and preservation of wholeness, of integrity, more than just *telling* the truth, it is *being* the truth, as in this is a *true* soul, a true person, so when that wholeness is threatened, Truth immediately knows. Understanding is the knowledge of the nature of things. But Wisdom is how to put them all together in various ways and how to use them! Finally, Peace is more than stillness, it is the sense of surety, of comfort, of all seven *because* they are all perfect in Goodness and together create eternal, mutual, self-supporting presence. Note that *all* these descriptions are nowhere dependent on a negative such as, Peace is the absence of fear, worry, anxiety etc. Goodness does not require evil to *be* Goodness!

All *this* is why evil has no win in us! Now to the Scriptures to give you a *written* witness to all this:

> Now I Paul myself beseech you by the meekness and gentleness of Christ, who in presence am base among you, but being absent am bold toward you:
>
> 2 But I beseech you, that I may not be bold when I am present with that confidence, wherewith I think to be bold against some, which think of us as if we walked according to the flesh.
>
> 3 For though we walk in the flesh, we do not war after the flesh:
>
> 4 (For the weapons of our warfare are not carnal, but mighty through God to the pulling down of strongholds;)
>
> 5 Casting down imaginations, and every high thing that exalteth itself against the knowledge of God, and bringing into captivity every thought to the obedience of Christ;
>
> 6 And having in a readiness to revenge all disobedience, when your obedience is fulfilled.
>
> 7 Do ye look on things after the outward appearance? . . .
>
> 12 For we dare not make ourselves of the number, or compare ourselves with some that commend themselves: but they measuring themselves by themselves, and comparing themselves among themselves, are not wise. . .
>
> 17 But he that glorieth, let him glory in the Lord.
>
> 18 For not he that commendeth himself is approved, but whom the Lord commendeth.
>
> (2 Corinthians chapter 10)

Surely Christians compare themselves to other men and that is the reason they do not believe the Scriptures that are right under their noses which tell them one can be perfect in this lifetime. They say, "Do you know anyone that is *perfect?*" "No, that's ridiculous. Only God is perfect, right?" "Right." "That's blasphemy if you think you can be perfect. You're not God." "Right, everyone *knows* this. Stay away from *that* guy. He's an anti-Christ. A devil." "Right. I asked my Pastor about it and he said the same thing." "Well, you should listen to him, then. Ours taught us about that last year. We're now all of the same mind just like the scripture says. Be of the same mind, right?" "Right. We follow the Word of God. He doesn't know his Bible, Right?" "Right."

Wrong. And I have the *author* of the Holy Scripture living inside of me. I don't need the paper and ink anymore because the Holy Ghost is closer to God than the Bible, and the Holy Ghost can do a whole lot more for me or anyone else than the Bible. And, oh, the Holy Ghost is the *meaning*, all of it, of the printed Word. You ought to think about that a bit, you hypocrites, vipers, full of dead men's bones, because it is dead men you follow, past and present, but the Holy Ghost which is always now, you refuse to accept, along with them who have Him!

However, if they considered that salvation is the Lord's work and not their own, and compared the feebleness of man's work to the power of God's work, then they would realize that God's work is always done in perfection. Then they'd believe that the Holy Ghost fights for the child of God the continuous battle against evil and always wins. I recall once again the prayer prayed by one who truly seeks righteousness, Lord, let me continually do righteousness, let me never sin.

Jesus said, No man can serve two masters, he will hate the one and love the other. You cannot serve God and serve the world. However, one reason why man feels confident even though he still sins is because he compares himself to those who seem to sin a lot more than he does. Thus he brushes off the *few* little things he feels he does wrong. Unfortunately, when one turns away from God through sinning, it doesn't matter by which sin because the result is still turning away. That is why Jesus made it plain to His disciples that there was no lesser or greater sin, but that, except they repent, they shall all likewise perish as do those that seemed to be great sinners. To this James also testifies, saying that whosoever shall keep the whole law, and yet offend in one point, he is guilty of all. Why? Because turning away from God is turning away from God no matter if it's to the right, left, or a *little* in between. One clarification, though, is that this does *not* mean all sins are the same in *depth* or *quality* of offense or harm. For instance, murder is more harmful and offensive than stealing, generally speaking. And unforgivable sins are more offensive and harmful than murder!

I shall now present even further proof that I am writing the truth. Paul gives other detailed descriptions of perfection in this lifetime. For example, in the following Scriptures Paul compares the sacrifices before Christ and their power to purify, unto the power of the sacrifice of Christ and the purification by the Holy Ghost.

> Then verily the first covenant had also ordinances of divine service, and a worldly sanctuary.
>
> 2 For there was a tabernacle made; the first, wherein was the candlestick, and the table, and the shewbread; which is called the sanctuary.
>
> 3 And after the second veil, the tabernacle which is called the Holiest of all . . .

6 Now when these things were thus ordained, the priests went always into the first tabernacle, accomplishing the service of God.
7 But into the second went the high priest alone once every year, not without blood, which he offered for himself, and for the errors of his people:
8 The Holy Ghost this signifying, that the way into the holiest of all was not yet made manifest, while as the first tabernacle was yet standing:
9 Which was a figure for the time then present, in which were offered both gifts and sacrifices, that could not make him that did the service perfect, as pertaining to the conscience;
10 Which stood only in meats and drinks, and divers washings, and carnal ordinances, imposed on them until the time of reformation. . .
13 For if the blood of bulls and of goats, and the ashes of an heifer sprinkling the unclean, sanctifieth to the purifying of the flesh:
14 How much more shall the blood of Christ, who through the eternal Spirit offered himself without spot to God, purge your conscience from dead works to serve the living God?
(Hebrews chapter 9)

For the law having a shadow of good things to come, and not the very image of the things, can never with those sacrifices which they offered year by year continually make the comers thereunto perfect.
2 For then would they not have ceased to be offered? Because that the worshipers once purged should have had no more conscience of sins.

3 But in those sacrifices there is a remembrance again made of sins every year. . .

12 But this man, after he had offered one sacrifice for sins for ever, sat down on the right hand of God; . . .

14 For by one offering he hath perfected for ever them that are sanctified.

15 Whereof the Holy Ghost also is a witness to us: for after that he had said before,

16 This is the covenant that I will make with them after those days, saith the Lord, I will put my laws into their hearts, and in their minds will I write them;

17 And their sins and their iniquities will I remember no more.

18 Now where remission of these is, there is no more offering for sin. . .

22 Let us draw near with a true heart in full assurance of faith, having our hearts sprinkled from an evil conscience, and our bodies washed with pure water. . .

(Hebrews chapter 10)

Where Paul says, having our hearts sprinkled from an evil conscience, he is speaking of having had sprinkled on the children of God that blood of Jesus Christ, which is the Holy Ghost, which Paul said, How much more shall the blood of Christ, purge your conscience from dead works to serve the living God? That blood of Jesus Christ is none other than the Holy Ghost because the Holy Ghost continually keeps one's conscience clean, being a continuous sanctification and guider into all truth, just as the blood of the flesh keeps the tissues thereof fully oxygenated. Therefore Paul pointed out that the sacrifices of old were not sufficient to clean man's conscience so that he would not continue to sin, but, then he pointed out that the blood of Jesus Christ, offered once, meaning also that it is sprinkled only once on a person, is sufficient to clean one's conscience from that time of sprinkling and forever after: For by one offering he hath perfected for ever them that are sanctified.

My question then becomes, Why then do Christians of all sects, including Catholics, sprinkle often the blood of Christ on the same people, who in turn confess to sinning often? Either these religious people have watered the blood of Christ down or they never possessed nor received that sanctification to start with. Why have they drug Jesus Christ's name back to the standard of animal sacrifices, which blood had to be offered often because it was not a pure enough sacrifice to clean a conscience? And where the conscience is still afflicted, there is recrimination from sin holding them captive, which *means* there is no forgiveness attained! Isn't that why Christians utter every Sunday that they are sinners, because they hadn't yet been forgiven? At least not by Jesus of the *New Testament!* Surely the blood of their transgressions and abominations shall be required at their hands in the Day of Judgment. Paul also chastened such as are now being chastened, and replied,

> 11 Now no chastening for the present seemeth to be joyous, but grievous: nevertheless afterward it yieldeth the peaceable fruit of righteousness unto them which are exercised thereby.
> 12 Wherefore lift up the hands which hang down, and the feeble knees;
> 13 And make straight paths for your feet, lest that which is lame be turned out of the way; but let it rather be healed.
> 14 Follow peace with all men, and holiness, without which no man shall see the Lord:

> 15 Looking diligently lest any man fail of the grace of God; lest any root of bitterness springing up trouble you, and thereby many be defiled... (Hebrews chapter 12)

How many have now been defiled by man's false religions? But the Holy Ghost is able to give one a clear conscience because he keeps one from sinning after He is received. The testimony to this is plain and it cannot be turned away, though out of stubbornness it may still be rejected even as the Pharisees stubbornly rejected Jesus Christ.

Now having thoroughly presented to my readers both reasoning and Scripture testifying that the grace of God, which is the Holy ghost, is given to make one perfect in this lifetime, I should now take some time to address two more Scriptures which Christians misunderstand to their destruction.

> For all have sinned and come short of the glory of God. (Romans chapter 3, verse 23)

True. All people *have* sinned and therefore have come short of God's glory. *Past* sinning before one is truly saved, meaning filled with the Holy Ghost. That verse does not say that all will *continue* to sin on this Earth nor that they will continue to fall short of God's glory. When Jesus places His Holy Ghost within a body and soul, He has placed his glory there, it says so in chapter 17 of Saint John verse 22,

> 22 And the glory which thou gavest me I have given them, that they may be one, even as we are one:
> 23 I in them, and thou in me, that they may be made perfect in one...

The next Scripture to examine is as follows,

4 And these things write we unto you, that your joy may be full.
5 This then is the message which we have heard of him, and declare unto you, that God is light, and in him is no darkness at all.
6 If we say we have fellowship with him, and walk in darkness, we lie, and do not the truth:
7 But if we walk in the light, as he is in the Light, we have fellowship one with another, and the blood of Jesus Christ his Son cleanseth us from all sin.
8 If we say that we have no sin, we deceive ourselves, and the truth is not in us.
9 If we confess our sins, he is faithful and just to forgive us our sins, and to cleanse us from all unrighteousness.
10 If we say that we have not sinned we make him a liar and his word is not in us.
(1 John chapter 1)

It is a wonder that with so many more Scriptures that plainly state the perfection God has to offer man, the Christians ignore them *all* and place their own foolish understanding into words that appear more obscure. For instance, the Scripture I just quoted, plainly states that God is light and in Him is no darkness, sin, at all. Then John states that if we say we are saved, which is fellowship with Christ, and yet still sin, walk in darkness, we are a liar and the truth is not in us because no darkness can exist within the light of God nor can darkness fellowship with light. Neither does darkness walk in light, but light drives away all darkness so that when we walk in the light of God we cannot sin! John is saying that when we live in such a state of perfection by being in God's light, it is the blood of Jesus Christ that continuously cleanses us from all sin. Why does John say, *cleanses,* and not *cleansed?*

The blood of Jesus Christ is that light which permanently and continuously drives away all darkness, thus making it so that our past sin is no more recalled because we sin no more, being holy. Why do you think Jesus said the Holy Ghost would teach us all things and lead us into all truth? Give us a *new* heart and *new* spirit. The old one is identified with failure but the new one with faithfulness. Thus His blood cleanses us from all sin and keeps our consciences clear both in the present and in the future. Since this light is continuous and our past sins are forever blotted out, that is why John says cleanses and not cleansed.

Which sin is cleansed? Obviously the darkness that was present *before* the light enters into a person, because no darkness can enter into the person once the light is in him and he is in the light. That is why John says, *all sin,* because the blood of Jesus Christ, which is Holy, cleanses us from *all* sin and no sin can enter into holiness. John is saying that if we walk in perfection then we know that the blood of Christ has sanctified us, which sanctification does not lapse.

However, Christians ignore all this in order to pervert the next verse, If we say that we have no sin, we deceive ourselves. However, John is simply saying that if we claim to not have past sin which needs continuous blotting out, then we are a liar. He's speaking to self-righteous people relying on their own judgment when God is the only true Judge, and His light is brighter, much brighter, than the best self-righteous soul ever. *This* is why Peter ended up denying Jesus Christ *three* times. Peter wasn't even exactly *self*-righteous. He was righteous truly but by the old standard which he felt pretty good about, ahh, until he denied Jesus three times because *that* was what it took to humble him enough to give up his whole will to receive the new one with a new heart and new spirit. He realized the old one just wasn't good enough. To make all this extra clear, John finishes with a reiteration in the *past* tense, If we say that we have not sinned. Even Simon Peter knew quite clearly he had sinned, but not only *that*, he was even more concerned about *why* he had sinned, and he realized his will was defective from the start! All it took was certain circumstances to arise and he would fail *even* what he loved most!

However, Christians claim that John is saying that if a person filled with the Holy Ghost claims that he no longer sins then he is a liar, *Worse* yet, Christians are not referring to just a finished sinful action but they are implying that some darkness or corruption still exists in a saved person because they say the verse refers to *having* sin, meaning some continuous corruption which leads one to sin. However, if this was so, then they are denying all the preceding verses as well as the understanding of God. What is even more ludicrous is, What then *is* the Christian's salvation? For every intent and purpose, a Christian's salvation differs nothing from being a common sinner who does not sin all the time but has excuses all the time.

Yet, the Christians further ignore the next verse which says that if we faithfully ask for forgiveness then Jesus will cleanse us from *all* unrighteousness. Why do Christians believe that being cleansed from *all* unrighteousness does not include the cleansing of the unrighteous *condition* that led to committing sin to begin with? Perhaps so they can simply justify themselves even though they are sinners, not saved, and a disgrace before God.

> He that saith he abideth in him ought himself also so to walk, even as he walked.
> (1 John chapter 2, verse 6)

～ THE FALL OF CHRISTIANITY ～

I conclude this chapter with a sense of satisfaction in knowing that its words give all glory to the Father, the Son, and the Holy Ghost. How can anyone who truly loves God not feel joy at words which edify Him. The Father, the Son, and the Holy Ghost are One God, the expression of the quintessence of eternal Life, Love, Justice, Peace, Understanding, Wisdom, and Truth. God is truth, being the sound foundation of the inner and outer workings of the whole Creation and beyond. God is Understanding because by Him was and is the various good natures of the whole Creation ordered. God is Wisdom because He knows how to implant and manifest His ways and knowledge into all things Created and made, from the Heavens, to the Earth, to the sea, to the creatures, and man, and how to make it all interrelate.

In order to have faith in this God which transcends all things known, one must believe in His totality. If one says he believes in the Father but does not believe in the Son, that person does not believe in God because God is either accepted in His totality or not accepted at all. If one believes in the Father and the Son but does not believe in Love, then he does not believe in God because he does not believe in the quintessence which is His Being, the I AM THAT I AM, which gives full meaning to the word *God*. Likewise, if one believes in the Father and the Son but does not believe in the Holy Ghost, he also does not believe in God nor has faith in Him because he rejects the Love and totality of the Living God.

You often hear Christian leaders, pretty much all of them I have seen or heard, say that the Trinity is a mystery. The *reason* it's a *mystery* to these vipers is because they *reject* the totality of God and so the Understanding that God absolutely loves to give is withheld from them by their own lack of faith! In God's Creative Writing, published *before* this book but *written* thirty years *after* this one as the Holy Ghost gave to me, well, it explains *clearly* the Trinity, what and how it really is and *why!* Because I have the faith to receive such Wisdom and Understanding which the Holy Ghost rejoiced for me to receive. It ain't based on what I read or on some other man's saying, but straight from the Holy Ghost itself. But wonder of wonders, it's also in the Holy Scriptures but *hidden* in plain sight in both the Old and New Testaments!

> But without faith it is impossible to please him: for he that cometh to God must believe that he is, and that he is a rewarder of them that diligently seek him. (Hebrews chapter 11, verse 6)

CHAPTER 5

EVEN PAUL SAID YOU CANNOT BE HOLY AND SIN

This chapter shall conclude the main message of this book. It shall allow the house of truth to rest, settled upon a sure foundation, impregnable to assaults and perversions. To the standard of writing any other book, surely I have clearly presented this book's subjects: real salvation and the true representation of God and His servants. To continue to make the same points might be deemed of belaboring the issue. However, this extraordinary message would not be complete if I do not point out how extensively the Holy Scriptures support the truth of this book, thus showing my readers how extensively religious leaders have ignored them.

It is necessary to challenge the religious misunderstanding of particular Scriptures, otherwise the understanding revealed in this book concerning Scripture might very well be countered in the minds of the religious by their misunderstanding. Therefore, this book is designed as a sort of inspection, verification, and demolition. The inspection of *many* things religion has implanted into hearts and minds, verification of what is weak and what is sound, and demolition of religion that goes against the Lord Jesus Christ, particularly Christianity, for this religion in its many forms targets those that have real faith in Jesus so as to freeze them in place upon Jacob's ladder so that they can't climb up any further. The poison inserted into Christianity eventually rots these people from the inside out.

When one inspects a bridge and discovers dangerous weakness that cannot be repaired then he warns everyone then seeks repair or destruction of that dangerous bridge. The demolition crew sets charges upon all of the main supporting points and blows them up so the bridge collapses. Otherwise, if the supports are not sufficiently destroyed, the results might produce an even more dangerous bridge than before. If the bridge cannot be sufficiently destroyed in one day then warning signs are posted on the remnants of the bridge so that no one drives off the edge into an abyss. What makes this task most difficult, though, is that the detractors and attackers of Christianity are many, *however,* they do so with pure hatred and mockery of our Lord Jesus Christ and the truth of both the Old and New Testaments. These attacks cause Christianity's defenders and followers to dig in deeper into the truth, but sadly, also into the lies that are rotting them from the inside out.

Do not confuse my motivations with those who hate God the Father, the Son, and the Holy Ghost. I desire Christians to become even stronger, but in holiness, not in religion. And I would rejoice greatly if they could seriously win their fight against the Lord's detractors, against the rising Beast which will soon decimate Christianity and Christians as a whole but not in a good way. The rising Beast will make the Roman's anti-Christian persecution look like Heaven compared to what the Beast is going to shortly do.

EVEN PAUL SAID YOU CANNOT BE HOLY AND SIN

As I mentioned earlier, there are a couple of points I will not be able to cover in this book because to properly cover them would require writing a book specifically on those points. God's Creative Writing addresses those points and delivers far more depth than this book. However, in this book is more than sufficient proof and warning that to try to cross the bridge of Christianity will inevitably plunge one into an abyss of no return with but one way out as they fall to their death. As they fall, if they cry out to Jesus and give themselves *completely* to His will leaving nothing held back, His presence will appear to them and quicken them in those instants so that they have time to accept and receive the Holy Ghost just before their bodies are destroyed. Unfortunately, the Beast is now rising quickly and many of their deaths won't be quick nor comfortable, and the Beast will employ all efforts to cause Christians to recant their faith. Please pay heed to the warning signs. What has been, will be, and is *now!*

How do I know what beliefs Christians use to try to justify their misunderstanding? I have talked to *many* Christians, leaders, and followers, and they always reveal what Scriptures they misuse when they attempt to justify a Christian's unholiness. They were taught this blindness from their leaders from generation to generation. Of all Scriptures, the ones in this chapter of this book I write are their favorites to abuse. The twisting of the following Scriptures, the last third of chapter seven of Romans, is foundational for Christian religious doctrine that is in great error. Unfortunately, they ignore the first two-thirds of chapter seven, chapter six, and the first third of chapter eight in Romans which with one accord contradict what Christians *think* Paul is saying in the last third of chapter seven of Romans.

I am going to begin with chapter six of Romans. I shall record it part by part and explain each part. Then I shall record and explain the first two thirds of chapter seven of Romans. After that, I shall record the Scripture that Christians stumble over. I shall then show how their understanding is wrong and present the first part of chapter eight of Romans which sums up the matter. Then I shall conclude with a testimony from Paul concerning how very deep is Jesus Christ's love for mankind.

In chapter five of Romans, Paul intimates how that after the law of God was given, sin abounded even more than before the law. The knowledge of right and wrong was made known to man, therefore, when one continues to sin, he not only maintains in his previous sin, but he also adds to that the blatant ignoring of what he knows to be right. Thus sin is made very sinful because he no longer sins in ignorance but willfully disobeys the truth of God to favor sin. This dynamic also tends to drive the sinner to even deeper and greater sinfulness. However, Paul continues to describe that even though man was so weak that he kept on sinning after he knew that it was wrong, even though sin was made more sinful after God gave his law to man, yet, God manifested to man even more mercy in hopes of saving him.

Wherefore, Paul concludes at the end of chapter five, That where sin abounded, grace abounded even more. That grace is the mercy of God, which includes the time to repent, and the eternal life of the Holy Ghost given to the truly repentant which enables man to keep himself from sinning and thus frees him from death, from the condemnation of the Law. For if you are forgiven of past sins and then you don't sin after that, then the Law can't condemn you! It's that simple. That straightforward. However, Christians go through elaborate contortions to propose a lie that doesn't even make sense. You would send your kid to their bedroom with no supper if they tried to propose such a poorly crafted lie!

Look, God is willing to remake the repentant through Jesus Christ so that they will not sin. That is why Paul says, that grace might rein through righteousness unto eternal life by Jesus Christ. The eternal life of being and doing only righteousness and not sinning anymore justifies God's kindness, His grace, to reign in us and through us. Grace reigns in us through righteousness, not through sinning, because sinning is not kind and not of Christ.

Yet, Christians believe that grace reigns in us through the crucifixion of Christ even though one continues to sin, as if the crucifixion is magical, producing an effect just because *what?* In this case the crucifixion causes God to go blind and can't see past the blood of Christ that actually *doesn't* do *anything* except blind God the Father! Actually, even in fantasy series there are *well thought-out* explanations to their worlds with actual energies and effects caused by their magic. Hmmm, Christians are generally not good fantasy writers, so maybe that's why their religion doesn't make sense.

Now God has always been righteous and has always reigned. Yet, it is not an external reign that is dealt with here in the purpose of the crucifixion, but His reign *within* a person, as Paul spoke about cleansing the *conscience*. Just because Jesus Christ overcame death and rose from the dead does not mean that death is overcome in *any* person. Only when that person receives the Holy Ghost of Jesus Christ is death overcome in him. Jesus Christ did *not* suffer to prove His own righteousness to Himself, nor even just to establish to the world that He is righteous, because there is no profit in establishing to the world that Jesus is righteous if a person must still be mastered by evil and *stay* mastered. Therefore, Jesus died so that we could live through His continuous righteousness and power *within* us. Otherwise, there is no profit from His death because the rule of grace would be conquered within a person by the rule of sin because *hiding behind the blood of Christ* does not stop sin from acting, *obviously*, because the person is still sinning, that is, according to the poorly written Christian doctrinal fantasy!

Unbelievably, though, Christians believe that the grace of Jesus Christ tolerates sin in them while they say they are saved from sin. That's pretty feckless, both in the opinion about Jesus and themselves! They think Jesus took all their guilt for sin away from them even though they still actively sin. Satan *loves* this kind of thing! Ha ha, your Jesus *cannot* keep you from bowing to me, says Satan! And looking at this even deeper, it says Jesus cannot purge nor purify *anyone* fully, so Satan says we will always serve him, not Jesus, because a little bit of corruption spoils the whole heart!

One must keep in mind that when he passes away from this world, whoever ruled over his internal state (God or Satan) at that point of passing away, he shall be accounted of the same master for eternity. When his master is judged for evil, so also are all of the master's servants, for they all willingly did his will and belonged to him. Still, a Christian's conscience tries to rebel against this truth, but Jesus said, Whosoever commits sin is the servant of sin. Yet Christians believe all are sinners until *after* they die and it is only *after* one dies that one is truly saved from evil. How can that be? If that was so, Jesus would never have had to come. God would have just waited for all to die in their sins and then been required to save all after they died. And since they all *died,* the blood of Jesus is not needed, for in dying their debt is paid, one way or the other!

Look! The requirement for blood sacrifice is enforced on the *living,* not the dead! Search the Scripture and see if *ever* God commanded a sacrifice for the dead. What difference then between those who

~ EVEN PAUL SAID YOU CANNOT BE HOLY AND SIN ~

supposedly serve God but sin and those who don't serve God but sin? What? That you believe Jesus will save you *in spite* of you not believing Jesus could make you perfect while you are still alive? Because while mortal you *have to* sin? Well then, everyone gets saved then *after* they die, even the unbelievers because they can just say they were ignorant, or made the wrong judgment on Jesus, but that's just a sin like many others that Christians make!

Paul perceived how that the devil might twist the thoughts of those who read the preceding Scriptures and cause them to think that the more one sins, the more grace would always come to save man. So Paul replies starting at the beginning of chapter six of Romans.

What shall we say then? Shall we continue in sin that grace may abound?

2 God forbid. How shall we, that are dead to sin, live any longer therein?

Paul is here clearly stating that there is an end to sinning in one's *mortal* lifetime, in that he says the children of God are dead to sin. To explain how and why, he continues,

3 Know ye not that so many of us as were baptized into Jesus Christ were baptized into his death?

Jesus Christ has always been alive and could never die. Yet, what death did Jesus die when He was crucified? He died unto the opportunity for sin to tempt Him while He dwelled in mortal flesh. After rising from the dead, He was no longer subject to the passions and temptations of a mortal frame. True, He rose with the same flesh body in which He was crucified, except for one difference. There was no blood in His risen body! He poured out all His blood at the cross.

Therefore, the risen life He lived on was strictly spiritual life in His flesh body! When one receives the Holy Ghost, one is receiving that Spirit which completely denied His mortal self even unto His mortal death in order to do the Father's will and thus Jesus died unto sin's opportunity to tempt. When one receives the Holy Ghost, one is also receiving through that Spirit everything which that Holy Spirit went through and established. That is why Paul then says,

> 4 Therefore we are buried with him by baptism into His death: that like as Christ was raised up from the dead by the glory of the father, even so we also should walk in newness of life.

If you are still sinning, or even believe you can't be perfect here in mortal life, you certainly do not fit within the newness of the risen Christ that Paul describes, *and* you have not died to your sinfulness predominately because you have *no faith* to receive such a blessing.

Once a person receives the Holy Ghost, that person's perceptions and judgments are guided by the Holy Ghost. To the Holy Ghost, the desire of the body of mortal flesh was denied even through to the death. Therefore the Holy Ghost guides the person, in which He dwells, to relate to his mortal body in that same fashion. Hence, the mortal body of flesh of a holy person is dead and buried unto himself by the Holy Ghost. Now, since that mortal body is dead to a holy person, yet, the Holy Ghost has born him anew, the Holy Ghost filled person then walks in the image of the Spirit of Jesus Christ's resurrection, to walk in newness of life. Yet, a holy person is required to dwell in mortal flesh and blood so that he may then obey the commandment of Jesus Christ which is to walk as He walked and do the same as He did when he was on Earth. Paul then continues to reiterate all the same points and indicates that when one receives the Holy Ghost, he not only receives the death of Christ, but also His Spirit of resurrection.

> 5 For if we have been planted together in the likeness of his death, we shall be also in the likeness of his resurrection:
> 6 Knowing this, that our old man is crucified with him, that the body of sin might be destroyed, that henceforth we should not serve sin.

Notice that the Scripture says, That *henceforth* we should not serve sin. The Scripture is saying that those who are baptized with the Holy Ghost have their former corrupted selves crucified and buried with the body that Jesus gave up and this destroys the body of sin, that henceforth we should not serve sin. However, the Scripture also says, That the body of sin *might* be destroyed. It says, *might,* because a Holy Ghost filled person still has to prove that he will hold to and follow the Holy Ghost. Otherwise, if he returns back to sin and brings up from Hell that which he had buried, the latter state of him is worse than his former state. Peter referred to this as, The dog returns to his own vomit and the sow that was cleansed to wallowing in the mire. Paul continues to emphasize,

> 7 For he that is dead is freed from sin.

Paul does not speak this verse to the sinner who dies a sinner because a sinner who dies a sinner is judged for his sin, *chained* by it, and is not therefore free. Paul speaks this of those who pass away in holiness and forgiveness, and from then on are not able to be tempted as would a sinner if a sinner could have a second chance after dying.

However, Paul is using the example of one who dies in order to describe the internal condition of one who has been saved by being baptized with the Holy Ghost. In truth, when one is baptized with that Spirit, he dies right then. He has to in order to receive the Holy Ghost. However, in that same instant, he is also born again with a healed body, a new heart, and a new spirit within him. The body looks the same as before but it has been cleansed of all ungodliness, the old self having been cast away by the Holy Ghost. As the old spiritual testifies, I looked at my hands, and my hands looked new. This is what Paul refers to as being dead with Christ and because one is dead to sin, then one has faith that he shall live. Speaking from experience, having actually experienced all this, I *know* it is all true. And it is not just faith that we will live by, but actually experiencing the Spirit of Life within, not just the mere flesh life and soul life before being filled with the Holy Ghost. Also, I experience the other six Holy Spirits of Jesus continuously!

> 8 Now if we be dead with Christ, we believe that we shall also live with him:
>
> 9 Knowing that Christ being raised from the dead dieth no more; death has no more dominion over him.
>
> 10 For in that he died, he died unto sin once: but in that he liveth, he liveth unto God

Paul is emphasizing that Satan, evil, death has no more power to condemn the souls of the holy children of God because Christ allowed Satan to take Him under once into death, but, being then raised from death, He left death behind. Death has no power over immortal life, only in the temptation of mortality. Therefore, Paul stresses in the following Scriptures that the holy children of God should look only upon that immortal Holy Spirit that they have received and believe that they are not mortal anymore, for Jesus said, He that is born of the Spirit is spirit.

EVEN PAUL SAID YOU CANNOT BE HOLY AND SIN

11 Likewise reckon ye also yourselves to be dead indeed unto sin, but alive unto God through Jesus Christ our Lord.

Satan desires to convince the children of God that evil can still master them. To apply his trickery, he tries to convince the children of God that since they still dwell in flesh and blood, they must bow to the lusts thereof as they had before Christ saved them. Satan even tempted Jesus Christ, so he certainly puts his holy children through all temptations. This is why Paul then warns that the holy children of God not allow themselves to be tricked into thinking they are still mortal just because they have flesh and blood. Paul stresses they are no longer of the mortal flesh but of the immortal Spirit of Jesus Christ and able to overcome all temptations and not sin. Therefore they ought not to believe Satan's lies that they must continue in sin.

12 Let not sin therefore reign in your mortal body, that ye should obey it in the lusts thereof.
13 Neither yield ye your members as instruments of unrighteousness unto sin: but yield yourselves unto God, as those that are alive from the dead, and your members as instruments of righteousness unto God.
14 For sin shall not have dominion over you: for ye are not under the law, but under grace.

By saying that they are not under the law anymore, Paul is showing that one does not have to depend on his own weak will to serve God, as they did in the past in order to try and keep God's Law. Man's will is known to fail, and when it does, they are condemned by the Law. However, God has provided through Jesus Christ a better keeper than the written Law of God which depended on prescriptive processes to pull the outside Law within one's soul.

The Holy Ghost is received when a person gives his entire will over to Jesus Christ. That person's will is given to His will and thus they are continuously guided into righteousness but from the inside out! Therefore, sin shall not have dominion over a person and one is no longer able to be condemned by the Law of God. One is no longer under the master of the written Law on paper, but under the Master of the Holy Ghost which is the *author* of the written Law of God. Outside-in internal processes of worship and servitude are replaced with inside-out internal processes. Thus the Scripture is fulfilled, I beheld the Lord always before my face that I should not be moved. Is there any kindness or favor imaginable that God could have done that is greater than that I just described? As Jesus said, The servant is not above his master but it is enough that the servant be as his master! Surely this is what Paul means when he says, For sin shall not have dominion over you: for ye are not under the law, but under grace.

However, Christians misinterpret that verse to mean that God did away with His Law and they then believe that grace means not holding one's sins against him *even though he continues to sin*. No Law, no sin! Poor, pitiful, misunderstanding souls. It's not the Law that God did away with, but only the method of keeping it! Therefore, sin that was before Jesus is still sin today, only more so, because the Holy Ghost gives man an even deeper righteousness to the depths of his innermost thoughts and conscience. Therefore, man is now guilty of his thoughts as well as his actions as Jesus pointed out that even if a man looks upon a woman to lust after her, he is guilty of adultery in his heart. Paul, being forewarned of the foolishness of man to come, writes the following rebuttal to the Christian's errors of thinking that breaking

God's Law after Christ is not deemed sinful as it was before Christ, and, that Christians can without guilt still sin while being under grace:

15 What then? Shall we sin, because we are not under the law, but under grace? God forbid.
16 Know ye not, that to whom ye yield yourselves servants to obey, his servants ye are to whom ye obey; whether of sin unto death, or of obedience unto righteousness?

Paul clearly describes the same final judgment for sin that was from the very beginning, death. Clearly, Paul has said here that as long as one continues to sin, he does not belong to God, but to the devil. He also is saying that those who belong to Christ do not sin. Because they do not sin, they are not able to be condemned by the Law. This is far removed from Christian's belief that Jesus did away with God's Law and thereby they are saved and not guilty.

Jesus said He came to fulfill the Law, not break it, or destroy it. Paul is saying that God has established the perfect keeping of this Law through the grace of God, which is the Holy Ghost. Doesn't this make a lot more sense, that the Holy, Almighty, Perfect God would make a way for man to keep *all* His Law, rather than God *changes His mind,* and says, Well, that's OK. You can keep sinning and I'll let you slide. Therefore, in Romans chapter six, Paul continues to show the difference between a sinner and a saint,

17 But God be thanked, that ye were the servants of sin, but ye have obeyed from the heart that form of doctrine which was delivered you.
18 Being then made free from sin, ye became the servants of righteousness.

Then Paul explains the reason why he still exhorts the children of God not to sin even though they be filled with the Holy Ghost, that is, because they still have flesh and blood. But, as they had in the *past* given their flesh over to corruption, *now* they have given themselves to holiness and dwell perfectly while yet still in the flesh.

> 19 I speak after the manner of men because of the infirmity of your flesh: for as ye have yielded your members servants to uncleanness and to iniquity unto iniquity; even so now yield your members servants to righteousness unto holiness.
> 20 For when ye were the servants of sin, ye were free from righteousness.
> 21 What fruit had ye then in those things whereof ye are now ashamed? For the end of those things is death.
> 22 But now being made free from sin, and become servants to God, ye have your fruit unto holiness, and the end everlasting life.
> 23 For the wages of sin is death; but the gift of God is eternal life through Jesus Christ our Lord.

This concludes the sixth chapter of Romans. A very clear and deep statement that there is no gray area between sinner and saint. One is either continually holy and saved or a sinner and damned. But Paul is not content to write just this message. He seeks yet more words from the Spirit of God and different examples to make the same points because the Spirit knows how man tries to duck away from God's word and slide in some justification to continue to sin, so we pick up now starting with Romans, chapter seven.

> Know ye not brethren, (for I speak to them that know the law,) how that the law hath dominion over a man as long as he liveth?

2 For the woman which hath an husband is bound by the law to her husband so long as he liveth; but if the husband be dead, she is loosed from the law of her husband.

3 So then if, while her husband liveth, she be married to another man, she shall be called an adulteress; but if her husband be dead, she is free from that law; so that she is no adulteress, though she be married to another man.

4 Wherefore, my brethren, ye also are become dead to the law by the body of Christ; that ye should be married to another, even to him who is raised from the dead, that we should bring forth fruit unto God.

The Law was given predicated on the facts that man is ignorant of much but also that man's will is too weak to keep it! So when he failed and broke the Law, he *knows* he has transgressed and then is required to make sacrifice to be absolved from the sin. The *requirement* of the Law is by man's *own will* he should freely keep it, and if broken, freely repent and sacrifice, for without sacrifice there is *no* repentance.

However, when even the *Author* of the Law came to Earth as a *mortal,* even He was subject to the Law. The legal reason why it says He was sinless is because He was perfect even while mortal and sinless because he kept *all* the Law, never transgressing it. But how did Jesus keep the Law? It wasn't by following commands! For the positive commands, Jesus simply followed what He *is*- Love. For the negative commands he simply followed what He *is*- Truth and Justice! However, when Jesus dies having kept all the Law, and *by the Law* it says if you keep *all* of it ye shall live, Jesus rises from the dead, but not just because He kept *all* the Law but because He is the *Author* of the Law being Life, and the other six Holy Spirits of God. When *we* are filled with the Holy Ghost we *don't* keep the New testament as if it were *Old,* by command as the Christians do. We also keep Old and New by Love, Truth, Justice, and finally Life! The same as Jesus did when here? Really? Why *else* would Jesus say, Do as I have done.

Now that the *Author* of the Law has risen in perfection, He now contains within Him the tried and tested absolute perfect Spirit to keep all the Law which governed *mortality!* He also fulfilled His saying, I am the way, the truth, and the life! That *way* is that no longer would God accept an inferior method of serving Him, that being sinning then sacrificing animals. Jesus did not *change* the Law, he changed the *method* of servitude and purification whose purpose was to make God's servants holy. The method, the purification, which is spiritually life giving, the truth, which is integrity and soundness, is all contained in the very same Spirit which fulfilled *all* of the Law while *mortal.* Thus the Holy Ghost of the Lord God Jesus Christ deepens his servants holiness considerably because when we receive and keep Him *inside,* we are *one* with Him! We are true and purified within His continuous oneness in us. Such holiness keeps us from sinning, for if we would sin after being filled with the Holy Ghost, there is no more oneness. No Christian is holy. *None.* At least not to the new standard of the New Testament. They tell you so every Sunday when they publicly confess they still sin, they are *still* sinners.

In essence, we are dead to the old ways of God's service and purification but even more alive to the Law of Justice, Love and Truth which is the *moral* part of God's Law. Jesus said that He came not to destroy the Law or the Prophets, but to fulfill their word. Thus, as long as a person lives, if he commits sin, he is judged guilty by the Law of God and condemned. If any person were to deny the true moral law of Love, Justice, and Truth from God and try and live by

EVEN PAUL SAID YOU CANNOT BE HOLY AND SIN

any other standard, they have gone a whoring after a false god, for there is no god beside the One Almighty God of Life, Truth, Peace, Love, Understanding, Wisdom, and Justice.

Paul's comparison is that of an adulterous woman taking in a strange man to be her protector, provider, and comfort. Yet, Paul says that if her husband be dead, then she is loosed from her marriage and free to marry another without guilt. Yet, there is no other God to marry one's soul unto, and to suggest one is guiltless if they cleave to any god but the true God is blasphemy. It is also blasphemy to suggest that God could die. However, Paul is not suggesting any of these.

God has always supplied the human being with a caretaker, a representation of Him, unto which man should marry his soul and thereby worship God. Before Jesus Christ, that representation, or mediator between God and man was the written Law of God, which in itself was a representation of the Spirit thereof, the Spirit of Truth along with the other six virtues of God. However, at the appointed time, it pleased God to send the very Spirit of the Law unto man but within a man thus enabling that Spirit to dwell with the population without them all collapsing! For the Jews of old, once they came out of Egypt, when they were at the Mount of God, had pled with the Lord God, Oh, let us not hear the voice of God again lest we all die! And God had said to Moses, They have well spoken what they have said. And then God promised to send them the Messiah, which is Jesus Christ, so that they could behold the wonders of Almighty God, and hear his words without being overcome by frightfulness. Thus God fulfilled His saying, Behold, I am married unto you, saith the Lord. To illustrate this further. I give the following example:

To order his affairs, a king daily sends out messengers to his subjects requiring his subjects to pay heed to the messengers he sent in the king's name. Yet, if the king sends his prince after he sent the messengers, the subjects will set the messengers aside in order to hear the prince because the prince is closer to the king and is more than just a messenger, being heir to the throne and one with his father's will. The prince is a more perfect communicator of the king's will, having, himself, authority and power. No crime is committed when the messengers are set aside for the prince, neither is there any adultery when one lays aside the written Law of God in order to follow the Spirit of God.

The word of the messengers is dead in the presence of the prince for it is delivered through mere servants. So also dead is the old method of serving God by using one's own mind and will to keep commands given by mere holy men, for a better way to keep God's Law is supplied by the Holy Ghost of Jesus Christ. Therefore, whoever would still yet favor to keep his own mind and will in attempting to follow lesser messages instead of having the Spirit of the will of God within them, those shunners of God's will are guilty of despising God; just as those subjects would be guilty if they desired to heed the messengers moreso than the prince, himself. The prince does not countermand the king's messages sent by the messengers, but the prince is able to bring the will of his father much closer to his subjects and produce even better loyalty.

After the prince is sent to dwell with the people, the method of sending messengers is dead by favoring a clearer mediator. Thus the people are required to fully give their hearts to this higher standard of living, otherwise they have insulted the king by despising his prince. Yet, there is even deeper understanding in this Scripture, Wherefore, my brethren, ye also are become dead to the law by the body of Christ.

Since Jesus Christ denied the body of flesh, in which is the selfish and lustful heart, and made that self dead unto the Holy Ghost, when one receives the Holy Ghost, his self is also dead and buried that he should be married to the Spirit of Christ. He is then dead to the law by the body of Christ because Christ's prayer was, Father, thy will be done, not mine. Therefore, no other self-will can exist in a person who has the Spirit of Christ within him since the prayer and fulfilling is always the same, Father, thy will be done, not mine. Since the written law required one to follow it with his own mind and will, when one receives the Holy Ghost he becomes dead to the written law of God because his own carnal mind and will are dead in favor of the glory and will of the Spirit of God within. This may sound repetitious but the reasoning actually develops the point with a different nuance. If it wasn't for the Christians being so blinded about this, any one of the various ways the point is made would be sufficient.

Instead of heeding written words outside a person and relying on self-interpretation and memory, one relies on the Spirit of God within, as Jesus said, the Holy Ghost, which is the Spirit of Truth, will guide you into all truth and teach you all things, and bring all things to your remembrance, whatsoever God has said to you. Ahhh, dear Christians, that description is way, way more than the Holy Scripture can do for you. Right?

I should like to explain one thing further. Man's will is still free even after he receives the Holy Ghost. In fact, it is freer than before he is holy because when one is a sinner, the evil spirit pushes, beguiles, tricks, compels, and outright forces one to serve it. When one is holy, the Holy Ghost comes with peace and lovingly presents one with opportunities and choices within the domain of goodness. It is a mistake to believe that because one's will only will allow him to choose goodness that, therefore, he is not free. Remaining in the domain of the goodness of God's will does not hinder one's freedom but rather enhances and embraces freedom. Why? God is Love and Love is free, being always freely given. No compelling. No forcing. No trickery. And anyone seeking perfect goodness simply does not resist the ultimate in goodness.

Thus one who belongs to the deepness of God's Love is deeply free indeed. Being of Love, the holy child of God freely offers his love to God and man. The real human being loves because he wants to more than anything else, not because there is some order or command that forces him, but because loving is intricate to what his being *is*, besides making perfect sense to embrace fully what you love. After all, within the *I Am that I Am*, Love is also intricate to *Being*. However, one who belongs to evil is dominated and oppressed from within and imprisoned by the chains of death.

God is only good, but, He is also the most free, and it takes one who is free to know the One who is Free. This is also why the two great commands deal with loving! Love requires freedom for love to be true. The natural man who hasn't been filled with the Holy Ghost is free to learn about everlasting life and live there, or he may explore the pit of death and exist in eternal suffering.

> 5 For when ye were in the flesh, the motions of sins, which were by the law, did work in our members to bring forth fruit unto death.
>
> 6 But now we are delivered from the law, that being dead wherein we were held; that we should serve in newness of spirit, and not in the oldness of the letter.

Unfortunately, Christians abuse these verses terribly, believing that their meaning is that they are delivered from the law because the *law* is dead! This is completely backwards understanding. Notice that

EVEN PAUL SAID YOU CANNOT BE HOLY AND SIN

Paul uses past tense, For when ye *were* in the flesh. Obviously they are still dwelling on Earth in flesh and blood but what then does it mean to say, For when ye were in the flesh?

Paul further indicates that when ye were in the flesh, sin ruled over them. Also indicated is that the Law of God determined what was and wasn't sin, and further, it determined a person's death because of the guilt of sinning. The body of corrupted flesh is yoked by the Law of God which prohibits the fruit of corruption that the self often yearns to bring forth. It was because of this corruption that the law was given and as long as such corruption exists, the law oversees its judgment. Yet, how then is one delivered from the Law while still in flesh and blood? The answer to these questions is right in front of Christian faces in the rest of the verse! That being dead wherein we were held. What's dead? *No* Christians. Not the Law! But the *self*, the body of sin is made dead by the Holy Ghost, by what *true* repentance does in fully turning away from all corruption. Together, in that spiritual marriage, the corrupted self no longer has power to hold one in sin, nor make one to sin, and therefore no power to hold one in condemnation. You see? But now we are delivered from the law, that being dead wherein we were held, that we should serve in newness of spirit! The newness of spirit is holiness which is brought to you by fully repenting, by you giving the Holy Ghost full permission to destroy all corruption within you! What then does the Law of God have to condemn within you? Nothing!

Also, this verse sets those two phases together, that being dead wherein we were held, that we should serve in the newness of spirit. They are together because they are *both* talking about our *internal* condition comparing being held captive by a will that *fails* but when it is replaced by a new one, we serve in newness of spirit. But Christians would have you believe that the verses are *not* comparable, that, well, the Law is dead so we are free. *How?* What *exactly* is the new *internal* condition that makes us free? The answer for Christians is *nothing!* They are free because outside of them the Law is dead and that mysteriously allows a new spirit in us? Which we *cannot* serve without yet still sinning? Makes no sense Christians. None at all. And here is another painful truth. You are completely unaware it makes no sense because you have allowed your leaders for generations to rob you of the simple ability to critically think, even to look honestly into yourselves and see the truth of how you work inside. As I said before, you are *trapped* in a Scriptural box where you substitute *endlessly* repeating Bible quotes for true thinking, examining, and real reactions to all that from an honest heart.

Take further note, dear Christians, That we should serve in newness of spirit, and not in the oldness of the letter. What does, not in the oldness of the letter mean? The processes used in the Old Testament in following *prescription* from the outside in. In other words, read the printed words God gave you and try to obey them. *That* is the oldness of the letter. Do you then see how serving in the *newness* of the spirit is a totally *different* process of worship having *within* you that *newness* where by you serve and glorify God? *Holiness from the inside out!*

> 7 What shall we say then? Is the Law sin? God forbid. Nay, I had not known sin, but by the law: for I had not known lust, except the law had said, Thou shalt not covet.

To some people, when they read about being delivered from the Law and see that it was not able to save them, they believe there was fault to the Law of God. Obviously, Paul is saying there is *no* fault

EVEN PAUL SAID YOU CANNOT BE HOLY AND SIN

within it. And, well, many people blame their own faults on God! Understand that there is no fault in God's Law but in people's weak heart, mind, and will to follow it, so that is why Jesus Christ had to come. Paul directly challenges these people by saying that the Law is not sin because it makes known what things are right and wrong to do and prohibits wrong actions. However, evil does the opposite. The evil spirit works through one's weak self to cause one to do those things which it knows are wrong for us and that by the commandments are condemned. Therefore evil takes the occasion by the commandments to condemn us, as the continuing Scripture describes,

> 8 But sin, taking occasion by the commandment wrought in me all manner of concupiscence. For without the Law sin was dead.

What does this mean, For without the law sin was dead? When was man ever without law? Even Jesus Christ submitted Himself to the Law. Only one man was without Law and that was Adam! Why? Because *Adam was the Law of the Earth* until the commandment came that he should die if he ate from the forbidden tree. Beside that single command which he was *subject* to, all else was subject to him. This is very important to note because the Christians confuse Paul's language by thinking that he is talking about himself when Paul is really speaking about Adam! And *then,* they draw wrong conclusions about the meaning of certain Scriptures. This becomes even more evident as the Scripture proceeds.

> 9 For I was alive without the law once: but when the commandment came, sin revived, and I died.

Paul was never alive without the Law, so obviously he is not speaking about himself, but is making a general statement about mankind to which the word *I* refers. Verse 9 of Romans chapter 7 reaches back to the very beginning of mankind, even to the first man Adam from whence we all came. But also, even the commandment not to eat of the forbidden tree was not in force *until* Adam broke that law because once broken *then* the consequences followed and yoked mankind to sin by breaking the first law. But before that, Adam was alive without the law because keeping that law did *not* give Adam life. The holy life was already there! *After* breaking that law, then they had to sacrifice for their sins to preserve the quality of their *mortal* lives.

Was that command given just so man could die? Absolutely *not*. It was there for mankind to mature and become wise, as wise as God! Huh? But they had to *break* the command to become that. No! No they didn't. In fact, in Scripture when God chides Adam and Eve, saying, Behold, the man has become as one of us, to know good and evil, God was mocking the foolish results of Adam and Eve's decision! The *lack* of Wisdom. Then how could they become *truly* wise like God from that tree without breaking the command? By meditating on it. *That's what it was there for.* What would it mean to disobey God? What *is* God? What kind of knowledge would result from disobedience? What does it *truly* mean that I am alive now? And God would have revealed to their understanding the truth of all that, without them *ever* even touching the forbidden tree! And they would have understood their free will and the power of goodness much better. So, the Tree of Knowledge of Good and Evil truly was *exactly* that, whether they ate from it or not. In *God's Creative Writing* the Holy Ghost in me goes into great depths explaining all this so the readers can see and feel the truth of it.

After the first law was broken, then God began making commandments to restore life to mankind, such as repenting and sacrificing animals so that *no one* could live *except* by the law. Also, at that time, the first prophecy from God about Jesus to come was given and *that* became part of the Law, too, so that the Law could truly embrace Life. As for the Scripture saying, For I was alive without the law once: But when the commandment came, sin revived and I died, the *meaning* of this is that death and sin had no power over Adam as long as he remained as he was made to be, that being holy with eternal life, thus, For I was alive without the law once. Adam's life was *not* given by the law before he broke it and that's why there were no sacrifices commanded of him *before* he broke God's Law. But, For in the day that thou eatest thou shalt surely die, well, when *that* command came into force, then, But when the commandment came, sin revived and I died. Revived? Because *Adam* was *ruler* over the entire Earth. Satan did *not* rule there *until* Adam gave it to him after Satan had already been rejected by God. Oh, what a revival! Satan felt quite emboldened by all the possibilities of *almost* totally destroying God's *most favorite and meaningful* creation! Yes. That's right. Most favorite and meaningful. This also is fully explained in *God's Creative Writing*.

So for all mankind, Adam's disobedience also led to the following commandment to which Paul was also referring, In the sweat of thy face shalt thou eat bread, till thou return unto the ground; for out of it wast thou taken: for dust thou art, and unto dust shalt thou return. Hmm, man became so wise. About as wise as the Christians are today without the Holy Ghost ever living in them. But let's continue with Roman's chapter seven so we can judge the full extent of Christians' wisdom.

10 And the commandment, which was ordained to life, I found to be unto death.

> 11 For sin, taking occasion by the commandment, deceived me, and by it slew me.

As all of God's commandments are, they are all designed to keep man's will to be one with God's will, to guide man not to separate himself from the God of Life. Hence, when God commanded man not to disobey Him and told man the consequences if he disobeyed God, this was indeed ordained (the purpose thereof) unto life. Yet, because the commandment makes known to man the way to live, the resulting breaking of the commandment condemns one to death.

Adam and Eve had *no* conception of death. They simply didn't take the time they should have to meditate upon what disobeying God would really produce, however, afterward, through the nine-hundred-plus years they suffered, they considered deeply and understood the life God had still spared them with. This is why Paul says,

> 12 Wherefore the law is holy, and the commandment holy, and just, and good.

And once more the following Scripture reiterates where blame and fault is found.

> 13 Was then that which is good made death unto me? God forbid. But sin, that it might appear sin, working death in me by that which is good; that sin by the commandment might become exceedingly sinful.

The knowledge of what is sin causes sin to appear as it is: evil, wicked, and condemned. The commandments give to man the knowledge that sin is death and therefore needful of repentance. The knowledge that sin is death makes known that sin is sinful. Sinning

~ EVEN PAUL SAID YOU CANNOT BE HOLY AND SIN ~

is made exceedingly sinful because sinning with knowledge is more grievous a violation than sinning through ignorance.

Again, I point out that the word *me* does not refer to Paul but rather to carnal man in general, all the way back to Adam, for we were all within Adam. Therefore, because all, even Paul, were contained in Adam, Paul uses the words, *I* and *me*. However, Christians believe that Paul is speaking of himself while being holy, after having received the Holy Ghost for some time, with a new heart and new spirit. Yet, Paul continues speaking of the carnal man by using the word *I*. Paul does this because he wants to make it very clear that all fault belongs to man and all goodness belongs to God.

14 For we know that the law is spiritual: but I am carnal, sold under sin.

The law, being from the Spirit of God is faultless, but, the self of man (which Paul refers to as *I* and *me*) is carnal because ever since Adam sinned, man's self has been separated from God, being sold out to sin to do that which is forbidden by God. From this point on, the Christians turn their stumbling into a complete fall off the cliff into an abyss by thinking that Paul is talking about *himself* instead of just the general carnal man. They reason within themselves that since Paul was saved when he wrote this and yet is confessing *himself* to be carnal, and in the following Scriptures of Romans *he* seems to admit to continued sinning, therefore Christians can be saved and yet still sin. Oh the confusion of the oldness of the letter. Why do you think Christians *love* this new misunderstanding? Hmm, I guess it allows them the best of both worlds? So they think?

Let me provide to the readers the *difference* between the Old Testament Levites and Priests who were *chosen directly by God* to minister to the Jews, and these New Testament *imposters* who chose themselves just like the jealous Jews vaunted themselves against Moses and were swallowed up by the Earth! The Priests and Levites of old were taught not only the *specific* letter of the word, but the direct meaning as *directly* handed to *them* by God. And, yet, eventually the people were corrupted, for even the perfect *prescription* handed down by God could not withstand Satan's attack on their weak wills. So what do you think Satan can do to these New Testament *imposters* who appoint themselves, create their schools, use their *own* schools and their *own* appointed officers to certify them as genuine so they *appear* to actually be valid? Well, that's really easy to know! Satan will have them teach the *exact opposite* of the truth! Judge for yourselves what the Holy Ghost in me is saying to you, dear Christians.

Let me be blunt, both with the Holy Ghost and the goodness He has now made me to *be,* Paul is not saying that he sins, but rather that the carnal man sins and that the *general* carnal self has no goodness in it. Surrounding the Scriptures the Christians use to err, is *exactly* the meaning just stated. Chapter six of Romans, and the first part of chapter seven, which we already covered, and the beginning of chapter eight that we are yet to explore, they *all* confirm the truth that was just explained that the holy children of God are dead to their carnal self and that it is no longer able to beguile them to sin. In Second Corinthians, chapter ten, as I cited in an earlier chapter of this book along with many other Holy Scriptures, Paul *clearly* describes that the Holy Ghost keeps him and all the children of God from sinning. I remind the readers with that Scripture again:

> 3 For though we walk in the flesh, we do not war after the flesh:

4 (For the weapons of our warfare are not carnal, but mighty through God to the pulling down of strongholds;)
5 Casting down imaginations, and every high thing that exalteth itself against the knowledge of God, and bringing into captivity every thought to the obedience of Christ;
6 And having in a readiness to revenge all disobedience, when your obedience is fulfilled.

Notice that Paul's obedience is full and the gift of the Holy Ghost first fights the battle against evil by bringing into obedience all thoughts of the one in whom the Holy Ghost dwells. Thus there is no room for a Holy Ghost filled person to sin. Or, would you prefer the words of Jesus directly from John chapter 17? That they may be one in us as thou father art in me and I in you. I in them and ye in me. Is there room to sin in there when we are in that oneness here on Earth? For Jesus speaks of what the Holy Ghost will do *here* which is *very clearly* described through the preceding chapters of John fourteen, fifteen, and sixteen. Look it all up if you are interested!

The ignorant, at best, believe that the Holy Scriptures have a few places in it in the New Testament where the Holy Ghost filled people did sin. With this in mind, I return to Romans to have my readers look at the rest of the Scripture through the understanding that it is supposed to have and not the lies the Christians have. Paul is also using the first person so as to speak gently to those he is writing to so that they might see in themselves that the situation of the carnal man is very wretched indeed. Perhaps if any are yet still carnal and read Paul's message, they would see themselves as wretched and repent and get filled with the Holy Ghost which upholds the good Law of God by causing one to keep it. Therefore

Paul also shows in the following example that the Law is good and worthy to be upheld.

> 15 For that which I do I allow not: for what I would, that do I not; but what I hate, that do I.
> 16 If then I do that which I would not, I consent unto the law that it is good.
> 17 Now then it is no more I that do it, but sin that dwelleth in me.
> 18 For I know that in me (that is, in my flesh) dwelleth no good thing: for to will is present with me; but how to perform that which is good I find not.

This is how I felt *before* I was filled with the Holy Ghost and the main reason I sought to receive it so that this *miserable* situation could be put to an *end.* Since then, I have experienced *exactly* as Second Corinthians chapter ten has described. But if ever there was Scripture dramatically designed to motivate others to truly become holy, it is that part of Romans chapter seven just recorded. However, true to 'good' Christian form, they have *perverted* the meaning to mean and justify the opposite.

Notice in the Scripture just above that Paul is making it very clear that he is talking only of the carnal part of man, (that is, in my flesh). Here he clearly describes the weakness of the Law of God in that it gives man a conscience to know when he does wrong but not a strong enough will to carry the conscience through to mastering the dumb flesh with all its lusts, For to will is present with me but how to perform that which is good I find not. Later, in chapter eight, Paul makes it clear that the Holy Ghost provides a way to overcome this weakness, even as Jesus described, The Father that is in me, he doeth the works.

~ EVEN PAUL SAID YOU CANNOT BE HOLY AND SIN ~

Romans chapter eight will show that Jesus Christ through the Holy Ghost gives a person more than just a conscience to know when one does wrong. The Holy Ghost of Jesus Christ becomes the way, the truth, and the life. Paul shows that the Law had already given man a conscience, but the Holy Ghost gives man the means to actually perform the good, and in fact, to *be* the good right here on Earth. The following from Romans chapter seven finishes up Paul's description of the carnal man who has only the written Law of God to fight against evil.

> 19 For the good that I would I do not: but the evil which I would not, that I do.
> 20 Now if I do that I would not, it is no more I that do it, but sin that dwelleth in me.
> 21 I find then a law, that, when I would do good, evil is present with me.
> 22 For I delight in the law of God after the inward man:
> 23 But I see another law in my members, warring against the law of my mind, and bringing me into captivity to the law of sin which is in my members.

First of all, take a closer look at the words of the Scripture just recorded. Sin dwelleth with me. Evil is present with me. Meaning *in* him. Hmm, does that sound like a holy person who has been purified, sanctified *by the blood of Jesus?* A law in my members bringing me into *captivity* to the law of *sin!* That overpowers his will, the will of his mind and also obviously of his heart because he says evil is actually put into *action,* it's performed. Does this sound like the new heart and new spirit of Jesus Christ? But pay close attention to *this:* For I delight in the law of God after the inward man. I'm sorry, but I know

Christians do *not* understand the full meaning of this because they have *never* actually been filled with the Holy Ghost and had a new heart and new spirit. That description from Paul *clearly* describes, not a holy person, but a man serving the Law of God under the *Old Testament*. In fact, the whole set of verses from verse 15-23 describes the *old* man under the Law of God.

Holy Ghost filled people do *not* delight in the law of God after the *inward man,* which means after their *own* will and conscience. That process describes Old Testament servitude. I, as a holy man, and other holy people have told me the same, that we delight in the *actual presence of the Lord Jesus Christ inside of us.* We also continually thank the Lord Jesus for the Holy Ghost and the *oneness* we have through the Holy Ghost with Jesus. There is *no* oneness with God in Paul's description except an Old testament kind of oneness but certainly *not* what the Lord Jesus describes, nor Paul, nor John, nor Peter, nor any truly holy person.

Clearly, Paul is not speaking of himself while being filled with the Holy Ghost, for he, *himself,* confesses many times that he is free from sin, dead to sin, does not serve sin, that *every* thought is brought into the captivity of the Lord Jesus, *not the other way around!* Paul says, Shall we continue to sin? God forbid.

Christians *foolishly* believe that the blood of Jesus 'covers' them so that when they continue to sin, that blood hides their sin from God seeing it. They also foolishly believe that Jesus took all their sins away simply because Jesus sacrificed himself on the cross, so that when Christians *do* continue to sin, it's whisked away before it can be counted. Never happened! Look, that is *not* the way purification works, not even in the Old testament. The blood that was sprinkled *actually cleansed* the Jews to the Old Testament standard. No better

∾ EVEN PAUL SAID YOU CANNOT BE HOLY AND SIN ∾

proof of that comes than the very fact that after they were cleansed they were able to actually *stand in the presence of God!* Had the process been some kind of Hocus Pocus like the Christians describe, then all the Jews would have *died* as soon as the Holy presence of God descended to them! That's what happens to corruption when it gets too close to God. Didn't you *read* that Christians?

So, as Paul puts it, how much *more* will the blood of Jesus cleanse your heart and conscience from dead works. Now this meaning is *very* clear, because Paul is talking about actual purification and *not* the foolishness of Christians perverted Hocus Pocus doctrine where ya still sin but it's just not seen nor counted. Besides, which is the greatest salvation, *Christians?* Your perverted doctrine or the truth the Holy Ghost in me just described? God *always* does the greatest good.

Paul thus concludes chapter seven by asking who shall deliver the carnal man from wretchedness and death. That doesn't sound like the description of holiness, does it? Serving God with the mind, but what he really means there is *intentions,* because his flesh obviously overpowers his mind, as he says, but with the flesh he serves the law of sin. Ahh, did God or Jesus *ever* mention *anything* that said merely serving God with good intentions was acceptable? But there is a hint even in these last verses of Paul's drama, that he means to guide people somewhere else. Who shall deliver me from the body of this death? The Lord Jesus Christ! Well, is Paul speaking about the rapture? No, not at all. He is speaking about truly living right, being holy *here!* Deliver me *here,* while I am on Earth. Let me let the Holy Scriptures *prove it to you!*

> 24 O wretched man that I am! Who shall deliver me from the body of this death?

25 I thank God through Jesus Christ our Lord. So then with the mind I myself serve the law of God; but with the flesh the law of sin.

Now Paul in the eighth chapter of Romans straightens up any confusion caused by his dramatic digression in acting out the carnal man. And by the way, these chapters are artificial, manmade decisions from Christian *experts*. The original is one *very* long Paul, ahhh, letter. That's important to understand because many folks will read, say, chapter seven and not even look at chapter eight. But in reality, the beginning of chapter eight is *directly* connected to and directly, *immediately,* follows what we just finished in chapter seven.

The beginning of chapter eight explains that all holy people of Jesus Christ are *not* carnal but walk *only* after the Spirit. How do I know he's talking about all Holy Ghost filled folks? Because he used the undramatic pronoun of *them*. And interestingly, that also proves that his dramatic use of the pronoun *I* and *me* and *myself* was never about him, but all carnal man because the word, *them,* refers to the only other full class of people- holy people! So here is the start of Romans chapter eight,

> There is therefore now no condemnation to them which are in Christ Jesus, who walk not after the flesh, but after the Spirit.
> 2 For the law of the Spirit of life in Christ Jesus hath made me free from the law of sin and death,
> 3 For what the law could not do, in that it was weak through the flesh, God sending his own Son in the likeness of sinful flesh, and for sin, condemned sin in the flesh:
> 4 That the righteousness of the law might be fulfilled in us, who walk not after the flesh, but after the Spirit.

Again, no condemnation to *them!* All people filled with the Holy Ghost. And this walk not after the flesh but after the Spirit is a whole lot more than just good intentions. *Walking* means actually putting into action what you are walking after, in this case the Spirit. But at the end of chapter seven Paul clearly describes walking after the flesh. So there is a huge change in meaning from the end of chapter seven to the very beginning of chapter eight.

Now, the Christians will still argue that it just means your sins are covered up, that you *can't* be made perfect. Almighty God just can't do that. *But,* think about it. If walking after the flesh isn't merely about intentions, but *actually* serving sin through full on actions with mind and heart being held captive, well, ahhhh, then, doesn't that also mean that *not* walking after the flesh but after the Spirit, and having *all* thoughts brought into the captivity of Jesus means that we are *not actually* sinning anymore because we are putting our *whole heart and mind and action* into walking holy?

And just like Paul had dramatically described *all* of carnal man, how the law of sin in the flesh held them captive to serving sin, well, he uses similar sentence structure in saying, For the law of the Spirit of life in Christ Jesus hath made me free from the law of sin and death. Well, because just like the effect of being ruled by the law of sin captures the whole person, so does being ruled by the Spirit of *life* in Jesus capture one's whole being! So the *meaning* of this is that holy people are free from the law of sin and death because they don't sin anymore! How else could one say they are *truly* free except it be honest holiness!

Why couldn't the Law of God give us the strength to beat all evil and be holy all the way through our conscience? Because once Adam destroyed mankind's perfection, well, it wasn't in mankind's power to rebuild it. We are not the author of the Spirit of God which Adam lost. But worse. Once Adam failed, evil ruled and dominated the Earth like never before. God had made Adam and Eve to live in Eden, in paradise, and to have dominion over the whole Earth with the power to keep Satan from gaining any foothold. But *not* the power to confront the devil having already a brutal rule! To acquire the goodness necessary to confront *that*, would mean that God Himself would have to make a *new* perfection specifically designed for such a challenge. *That* is what this verse is describing: God sending his own Son in the likeness of sinful flesh, and for sin, condemned sin in the flesh.

The meaning of that verse is incredibly profound. Jesus enters mortality and *experiences* all the weakness and all the pains and all the sufferings of mortality. He is *tempted* by evil in *all* ways mankind could be tempted. What is Jesus response to all of this? He creates strength within *mortality* that never existed here before! But not just strength, but faith, wisdom, understanding, all that is needed to be holy here on Earth while *mortal*, no matter how hard it gets *including* going through death! And all that never existed here before. And for sin, condemned sin in the flesh, while being mortal! What better way to condemn sin in the flesh than to make a new heart, a new spirit *within* mortality that can keep us holy *in mortality*? Because Jesus rose with *all* that newness He created here in mortality *specifically* so He could give it back to us to live by, right here in mortality! That the righteousness of the law might be fulfilled in us, who walk not after the flesh, but after the Spirit.

Somehow, Christians believe that they can walk after the Spirit of Christ and yet still sin. They have been poisoned from almost the time when Jesus left. That huge body of *believers* mentioned in the

~ EVEN PAUL SAID YOU CANNOT BE HOLY AND SIN ~

Holy Scriptures were believers but *not* holy. Once the holy people were killed off along with the most serious believers, for they were the ones who were willing to be thrown to the lions, tortured, and other horrendous things because they refused to recant Jesus name, then the rest ended up forming Christianity as we know it today! Without the knowledge of the Holy Ghost, these *believers* did the best they could but unfortunately that also included *a lot* of justification for being saved while they *still* sin. Satan was able to leverage *that* poison into the doctrine they developed.

So now, Christians are walking after the *wrong* spirit at least part of the time, and only *half-walking* after the Spirit of God the rest of the time. How is that possible? Because their sincere faith allows the Holy Spirit to dwell *with* them, but they keep Him from dwelling *in* them continuously. But depending on the individual, how much they can disbelieve the poison, the Holy Spirit can come and go, even in and out of the person but not stay inside. As Jesus said, I dwell with you but shall be in you to abide with you forever. That forever in you only happens when you give your whole will up and receive the Holy Ghost. The *I dwell with you* phase is designed to lead the individual *personally* into the *I dwell in you*. Unfortunately, *that* is what the poison prevents. So you can walk into any serious church, feel the presence of the Holy Spirit, and by virtue of what they all feel, they all believe they are saved, *truly* saved, but yet still sin! Psychologically, this dissonance produces *many* problems!

To walk after the Spirit of Jesus Christ, who is the Spirit of the Law, is an even more narrow road then when man just walked by the written Law. However, somehow Christians think the road of the Spirit is *broader* and allows them to sin and be justified. Obviously, this is grossly mistaken because Jesus even condemns one's thoughts and feelings and makes us guilty when these are wrong. The written law did not outwardly condemn a man if he lusted after a woman, but since Jesus Christ came, he said that whosoever looketh upon a woman to lust after her is guilty of adultery in his heart. This is also true for anger and the unmerciful, for the written Law did not condemn those who were angry with their brother in his heart. All Satan has to do is maneuver you or simply wait till the Holy Spirit is being held away by your own, old, weak will, and then the devil can slip things into you that you don't want and even make you do what you don't want to do. Then you feel guilty, then you sincerely call the Holy Spirit more deeply to you, and the cycle repeats, and repeats, and repeats, which produces *exactly* what you see today!

Christians don't even realize they are calling Jesus Christ a liar because they say that His Holy Ghost filled children still sin, minding those things of the flesh and self. Jesus prayed unto His Father in John chapter seventeen,

> 15 I pray not that thou shouldest take them out of the world, but that thou shouldest keep them from the evil. They are not of the world, even as I am not of the world.

However, Christians do not believe that God answers the prayers of His only begotten Son. Christians overlook the meaning of, But that thou shouldest keep them from the evil, which means that they would not sin, not that evil wouldn't attack them, because Jesus had already told them how badly they would be treated.

Surely God answers Jesus Christ's prayers and Christ never asked for anything in vain nor halfway nor lukewarm. In fact, Jesus told man to ask for goodness in His name and believe it shall be granted unto him, and it *shall* be done for him by God. Are Christians saying that Jesus Christ did not believe in His own prayers? OK. Then here is Paul, you Christians *love* Paul, right? The continuation of Romans chapter eight,

> 5 For they that are after the flesh do mind the things of the flesh; but they that are after the Spirit the things of the Spirit.
> 6 For to be carnally minded is death; but to be spiritually minded is life and peace.
> 7 Because the carnal mind is enmity against God: for it is not subject to the law of God, neither indeed can be.
> 8 So then they that are in the flesh cannot please God.
> 9 But ye are not in the flesh, but in the Spirit, if so be that the Spirit of God dwell in you. Now if any man have not the Spirit of Christ, he is none of his.

Here it is, But ye are not in the flesh, but *in* the Spirit, if so be that the Spirit of God dwell *in* you. The Spirit of God insulates the person who is inside the flesh body so that the carnal self can no longer touch that person to compel him to sin. The will of God in the Holy Ghost is stronger than the will of carnal man, and so if a man denies himself completely for Jesus Christ, at that moment the Holy Ghost comes very close to him, allowing him to feel the presence of Jesus like never before. Then, because by that greater Light the man sees himself even more clearly, if he finishes denying *all* of himself and *then* opens fully to just the presence of Jesus that is now so close to him, at that moment the Holy Ghost will come into him to stay, abiding in him forever.

> 10 And if Christ be in you, the body is dead because of sin; but the Spirit is life because of righteousness.

11 But if the Spirit of him that raised up Jesus from the dead dwell in you, he that raised up Christ from the dead shall also quicken your mortal bodies by his Spirit that dwelleth with you.

Even ones mortal body is quickened by the Spirit of God so that it does not move about because of its own will but because of the will of the Holy Ghost, the Holy ghost having the mastery over dumb flesh. That is why when Paul was stoned to death, he didn't die, but got back up and walked away! It wasn't his time to depart and the Holy Ghost picked his body back up and he went about his Father's business. After all, through Paul, the dead were raised, so, makes sense such power would raise him!

The destruction of the main supports of the poison in Christianity have now been completed. By now it should be clear that Christianity is condemned by Jesus Christ as are *all* religions because none of them are holiness. They are prescriptive but the Holy Ghost is the actual presence of Jesus inside holy people, a *state* of holy consciousness, if you will allow me such a clear and accurate description! In a way, Christianity is the same thing that the Pharisees had, who gave Christ up to be crucified. That which has been is that which shall be, and, That which hath been is now.

I will tell you, I have been thrown out of churches for basically saying what Jesus said, that the Holy Ghost is our only true leader, that only He can teach us all things and lead us into all truth, but from the inside out. Jesus *did not* say the Holy Bible would do that, nor can it, for the Holy Ghost is the *Author* of the Holy Scripture, the true Word of God, being Spirit, *not the paper and ink*. The Holy Scripture is just a true witness, a *partial* witness at that, but it is *now* not meant to

EVEN PAUL SAID YOU CANNOT BE HOLY AND SIN

guide us, nor lead us, nor can it keep us, *especially* now with the Beast rising and hell bent on destroying us. But the poison in Christianity *forces* you to believe that the Bible is the Word of God because, since the Holy Ghost is *not* constantly in you, you feel you need *something* to constantly hold on to, so you *choose* to elevate the *printed* word of God, which Paul even said was a mere shadow of the Holy Ghost. So you are *forced* by Satan to lie about what the Bible is and what it can do! Because you have that dissonance between you and the Truth that I just described a bit ago! *Please* wake up. I don't want to see happen to you what I *know* will happen if you don't heed this message.

Even the Jews of old knew better than what you do now, better than to think the written word was all there was to serving God! As it is written, For what nation is there so great, who hath God so nigh unto them. . . and what nation is so great, that hath statutes and judgments so righteous as all this law. . . In other words, the actual *presence* of God was known to be with His chosen people *along with* the Holy Scripture. Unfortunately, that presence is more and more scant with Christians and their churches, and every day now, Satan leverages your dissonance with the Truth to drive your churches even now into actual perversity which *supports* the rising Beast!

The truth offends the leaders in churches who want to insert themselves between you and God. I have now been holy for thirty-one years and the Lord has guided me to help others receive the Holy Ghost. My heart is filled with joy for them, to see them able to walk freely, independently of all mankind having the true guider within them that Jesus Christ died for us to have. All of them can't stand these imposters with their college lecture type preaching lulling their followers to sleep. They all grieve for the people being so misled as lambs to the slaughter, but *not* a good sacrifice.

～ THE FALL OF CHRISTIANITY ～

To conclude this chapter, I would like to record two Scriptures which testifies of Jesus Christ's great love for man, even while man was yet still a sinner.

> 5 And hope maketh not ashamed; because the love of God is shed abroad in our hearts by the Holy Ghost which is given unto us.
> 6 For when we were yet without strength, in due time Christ died for the ungodly.
> 7 For scarcely for a righteous man will one die: yet peradventure for a good man some would even dare to die.
> 8 But God commendeth his love toward us, in that, while we were yet sinners, Christ died for us. (Romans chapter 5)

Shortly before Jesus was taken to be crucified, Jesus prayed to God His Father as follows,

> 19 And for their sakes I sanctify myself, that they also might be sanctified through the truth.
> 20 Neither pray I for these alone, but for them also which shall believe on me through their word;
> 21 That they all may be one; as thou Father, art in me, and I in thee, that they also may be one in us: that the world may believe that thou hast sent me.
> 22 And the glory which thou gavest me I have given them; that they may be one, even as we are one:
> 23 I in them, and thou in me, that they may be made perfect in one; and that the world may know that thou hast sent me, and hast loved them, as thou hast loved me.
> 24 Father, I will that they also, whom thou hast given me, be with me where I am; that they may behold my glory, which

thou hast given me: for thou lovest me before the foundation of the world.

25 O righteous Father, the world hath not known thee: but I have known thee, and these have known that thou hast sent me.

26 And I have declared unto them thy name, and will declare it: that the love wherewith thou hast loved me may be in them, and I in them. (John chapter 17)

CHAPTER 6

PERVERTS (SODOMITES) JESUS SAID . . .

I would have preferred to end this book with the previous chapter, however, the provocation against God committed by the religious has reached to the ultimate offense. The setting up of abomination where it *ought not to* be has also occurred in times past and God's response has always been the same: The abominations and all those supporting it were destroyed whether it was a city, nation, land, or the whole world.

Now I must warn you before you read any further because I don't treasure up wrath unto the Day of Judgment, just like Paul warned against. I prefer mercy to the repentant. And I even understand the Lord Jesus is *very* patient, so patient, in fact, that he will even let the whole world go to Hell, waiting for the very last soul to come in, just like He did in the days of Noah. But *this* day isn't the same *season* as Noah, even though Jesus said it would be *like* Noah's day, and *as* Sodom's day.

Except for one little detail: Except those days should be *shortened*, there should no flesh be saved. For in those days there shall be affliction like never before nor ever shall be. What does this mean? Well,

THE FALL OF CHRISTIANITY

while the foolish Christians are busy *copycatting* or, as they like to say, *imitating* Christ, meaning, acting just like they did, in their *estimation* from all their scholars, trying to act just like they did in the *season* when Jesus and the disciples were here, well, while the Christians are back in *that* season, time has passed them by and we are in a totally *different* season, one that many have been lied to about and told they will never see! They call these fools pre-tribers because they think Jesus is going to pluck them off the Earth *before* the Beast takes over. He's taking over right now.

What does it mean that we are in a different season? Well, that gets me back to my warning which I am about to describe. This book explains *clearly* the weakness of Christianity and why it is rejected by the Lord Jesus Christ. But because of all those weaknesses it will be *completely* unable to stand against this rising Beast described in Revelation. Christians are feckless, powerless, and weak, with very little to *none* of the Lord Jesus presence with them. But *holy people* filled with the Lord God Jesus Christ's Holy Ghost are, in *this* season *not* powerless at all. And some of us, as is described in Revelation and Daniel, well, there is a reason why Jesus said, It is better for you to have a millstone hung about your neck and cast into the sea than to offend the *least* one of His holy children.

So I am now warning the readers who will take offense at this book, or at the videos the Lord Jesus gave me at www.faithwalkerseries.com or anything in The Faithwalker Series, or offense at anything I post on X. If you want to do me harm, come on and try. I won't harm you. Well, wait. I should be clear on this. By man's weapons nor force from this body, I will not hurt you. I give you my word. But if you try to hinder or harm me or anyone dear to me, you will wish you had never been born. And *that* is just what will happen to you

PERVERTS (SODOMITES) JESUS SAID...

before you end up in the Lake of Fire that burneth with brimstone for eternity. Now if you want to find out what Brimstone really is, read God's Creative Writing. These paragraphs you just read, they weren't in the original manuscript thirty years ago. Well, I've grown a bit deeper in the Holy Ghost since then. Please. Please don't cut *your* days short when you can have a little more time to revel in your debauchery before you go to Hell.

In the Old Testament one finds that the abominable crept in and took over the temples that were supposed to be holy, where upon when a righteous king took rule, he destroyed those people. Of all sinners, it is the ultimately perverse who are responsible for angering God so, until God Himself came down within the angels to see *directly* how evil Sodom had become. And then He burnt the cities *completely* up. Yet, even with all this warning, the world has fallen to that base standard once more. But only *once* more, because after this time there will be no more.

Perverts are claiming that the Holy, Almighty God, in whom is all Wisdom, Understanding, Love, Life, Truth, Peace, and Justice, made them to be what they are. Is it wise for the same sex to be profane with the same sex? Is it wise to believe that if you are genetically one gender, that you are really the other? Is it wise to *choose* to pervert God in your understanding or to fault Him rather than admit that you are perverted or at fault? Is it understanding to pervert the use of your reproductive organs? Is it love to be made into a confusion? Regrettably, some come to their senses far too late. The damage is done.

When God placed the seed of life of man within his body, did not God place it there to be sown in fertile ground so that if it be God's will, it should grow? How then do perverts accuse God of giving them seed to plant into ground from where it could *never* grow?

God is not self-destructive, neither is he able to make anything to be self-destructive for then would God violate the Love that he is. It is impossible for God to have made any man with desire to mate with anything except to mate with the woman with whom he was made to mate. Perverts are accusing the Almighty, all Wise God of giving them body parts that are specifically designed for one purpose, yet, they say God gave them a desire to use them for that which is not that purpose.

Who is confused here, man or God? Who is the liar here? It is impossible for God to lie but man lies from his early youth on up. When a man or woman changes themselves so that they no longer have the natural desire that God made them to have, and, when they place in themselves the unnatural desire unto self-destruction that God could not have given them, then they have destroyed themselves completely because they have changed God's making, by their own free will. This is suicide and suicide is not forgivable.

Many people might say, But look at all the good things that perverts do. I ask these foolish people, is it good to promote 'life' which is not the making of God? That is why one-third of the angels were cast out of Heaven, because they followed Lucifer, the one who changed his making into something that God didn't make. Those angels were thinking about all of the goodness that Lucifer had and was doing. Was it goodness in the eyes of God? Obviously not.

Now I am *not* trying to persuade the perverts. No. Their time is already appointed, unchangeable. But those who are *not* perverts, even those who still have a conscience that is now *really* beating them up badly because they have been into some really bad stuff- well, just because for whatever reason- but now they've turned fully away and find they still have some natural feelings left for the right attraction, also, to those who never got into that at all but who are compassionate people and feel sorry for the downtrodden and loathe to be haters, I say unto you all, think a little deeper. There are *seven* Holy Spirits of God as *One*. For a good reason. Because *none* of those seven can truly be what they are if but even *one* of them is missing from the others. Go ahead. Try and imagine it.

Can Love be Love without Justice? When Love becomes unfair, it is no longer Love. Nor is it Love if it doesn't embrace Life, or the others mentioned. Those seven, Life, Love, Peace, Justice, Truth, Understanding, Wisdom make up the very essence of Reality. They are like a seven-sided gem, each facet unique, but all part of the same stone. Look into one deep enough and you see the other. So I say unto all those who are *not* perverts but still support and love them, What do you have to lose? Try the meditation. Pick one of the seven then remove just one of the others and see if the one you picked can remain true! They would all self-destruct. And *that* is *precisely* what you are doing to yourselves in supporting the perverse and thinking you are doing the right and good thing. God will hold you guilty just as he holds the perverse guilty. This has already happened in Judges chapters nineteen and twenty.

Many sins may be committed but after they're done, they're past and forgivable. However, perversity is a sin that changes a person's making so that he will *continually* embrace that sin. A continual *state* of sin is not forgivable because a person cannot say, Forgive me for what I have done. One surely can't get forgiveness by saying, Forgive me for what I am doing and going to *keep doing, keep being,* since while you ask for forgiveness, you *know* it is wrong but continue to do it anyway. That's not true repentance, is it? And if some want to take issue with me describing perversion as a continual *state* of sin, well, I just take them at their own words to describe themselves. Don't they say, *It's an orientaaaation!* Right? Well, that's a *continuous* conscious state of sin. But the point of this chapter is to show people that all these things are written in the Holy Scriptures of the *New Testament!*

I have heard many religious people say that condemnation of perversion was only in the Old Testament, and that Jesus never said anything about perversion. These people are lying and this chapter shall prove that Jesus Christ was very clear on such things, and so also is Jesus Christ's Holy Ghost clear on the condemnation of such beastly abominations. To start with, let me give to the religious the words that the Holy Ghost gave to Paul concerning such a matter. Realize that Jesus Christ is Love and that is why He condemns perverts to destruction.

> 16 For I am not ashamed of the gospel of Christ: for it is the power of God unto salvation to every one that believeth; to the Jew first, and also to the Greek.
>
> 17 For therein is the righteousness of God revealed from faith to faith: as it is written, the just shall live by faith.
>
> 18 For the wrath of God is revealed from heaven against all ungodliness and unrighteousness of men, who hold the truth in unrighteousness;
>
> 19 Because that which may be known of God is manifest in them; for God has shown it unto them.
>
> 20 For the invisible things of him from the creation of the world are clearly seen, being understood by the things that are made, even his eternal power and Godhead; so that they are without excuse.
>
> 21 Because that, when they knew God, they glorified him not as God, neither were thankful; but became vain in their imaginations, and their foolish heart was darkened.

~ PERVERTS (SODOMITES) JESUS SAID... ~

22 Professing themselves to be wise, they became fools,

23 And changed the glory of the uncorruptible God into an image made like to corruptible man, and to birds, and forefooted beasts, and creeping things.

24 Wherefore God also gave them up to uncleanness through the lusts of their own hearts, to dishonour their own bodies between themselves:

25 Who changed the truth of God into a lie, and worshiped and served the creature more than the Creator, who is blessed forever. Amen.

26 For this cause God gave them up unto vile affections: for even their women did change the natural use into that which is against nature:

27 And likewise also the men, leaving the natural use of the woman, burned in their lust one toward another; men with men working that which is unseemly, and receiving in themselves that recompense of their error which was meet.

28 And even as they did not like to retain God in their knowledge, God gave them over to a reprobate mind, to do those things which are not convenient;

29 Being filled with all unrighteousness, fornication, wickedness, covetousness, maliciousness; full of envy, murder, debate, deceit, malignity, whisperers,

30 Backbiters, haters of God, despiteful, proud, boasters, inventors of evil things, disobedient to parents,

31 Without understanding, covenant breakers, without natural affection, implacable, unmerciful:

32 Who knowing the judgment of God, that they which commit such things are worthy of death, not only do the

same, but have pleasure in them that do them. (Romans chapter 1)

Notice that the Holy Ghost of Jesus Christ is upholding God's judgment of perversion and describes quite clearly unto what God has given those people over. Now, since God has given those people over to nothing but wickedness, I'd like to know where those perverts are going to find goodness, since they lie and say they have plenty of goodness in them. When God says he gives one over to wickedness, it is impossible for that person to turn and take of the goodness of God because God has withholden goodness from him, and Almighty God cannot be overpowered.

Some might think this sounds unfair but that's because they have no understanding. The perverse turn against knowledge and goodness at such a base level that even animals don't rebel against their making like *that*. Like in the days of Noah when every imagination of the thoughts of their hearts was only evil *continually*, once human's reach such a level of evil, by *design,* goodness can no longer be accessed by them. What does that mean?

It means, basically, they have turned themselves into human beasts the same way Lucifer turned himself into the devil. A self-destruction of the spirit that leaves that spirit without goodness. Meaning, a conscious existing evil and death! It is *impossible* for such to choose any goodness at all for goodness sake because evil simply can't choose good. It may seem like they choose goodness, as even Satan *loves* to tell people the truth! That seems like goodness, doesn't it? But when he can use that truth to destroy them. So it's truth, but with a little twist of evil attached. Truth for the sake of evil isn't truth. Truth is more than just not telling lies.

Also, when things get rough, hard, *miserable* for the wicked, they often want to turn to good, to choose good. However, that's not because they love good but because they want to escape their suffering. Many times Justice will withhold all goodness from them because that is Just! But if you would like to argue with God over this, then help yourself. The world would be better without you, anyway, if you really think you can raise your so called goodness over God's Goodness when all of it is His from start to finish.

Jesus said He came to fulfil the Law of God and not to change any of it. That is why Jesus Christ casts the Beast and the false prophet into the Lake of Fire that burns with brimstone for eternity. Perverts are part of that Beast according to the word of the living God. Who doesn't believe that? Then listen to the Holy Ghost through another holy child of God, Peter,

> But there were false prophets also among the people, even as there shall be false teachers among you, who privily shall bring in damnable heresies, even denying the Lord that bought them, and bring upon themselves swift destruction.
>
> 2 And many shall follow their pernicious ways; by reason of whom the way of the truth shall be evil spoken of.
>
> 3 And through covetousness shall they with feigned words make merchandise of you: whose judgment now of a long time lingereth not, and their damnation slumbereth not.
>
> 4 For if God spared not the angels that sinned, but cast them down to hell, and delivered them into chains of darkness, to be reserved unto judgment:
>
> 5 And spared not the old world, but saved Noah the eighth

person, a preacher of righteousness, bringing in the flood upon the world of the ungodly;

6 And turning the cities of Sodom and Gomorrah into ashes condemned them with an overthrow, making them an ensample unto those that after should live ungodly;

7 And delivered just Lot, vexed with the filthy conversation of the wicked:

8 (For that righteous man dwelling among them, in seeing and hearing, vexed his righteous soul from day to day with their unlawful deeds);

9 The Lord knoweth how to deliver the godly out of temptations, and to reserve the unjust unto the day of judgment to be punished:

10 But chiefly them that walk after the flesh in the lust of uncleanness, and despise government. Presumptuous are they, selfwilled, they are not afraid to speak evil of dignities.

11 Whereas angels, which are greater in power and might, bring not railing accusation against them before the Lord.

12 But these, as natural brute beasts, made to be taken and destroyed, speak evil of the things that they understand not; and shall utterly perish in their own corruption;

13 And shall receive the reward of unrighteousness, as they count it pleasure to riot in the daytime. Spots they are and blemishes, sporting themselves with their own deceivings while they feast with you;

14 Having eyes full of adultery, and that cannot cease from sin; beguiling unstable souls: an heart they have exercised with covetous practices; cursed children. . . (2 Peter chapter 2)

PERVERTS (SODOMITES) JESUS SAID...

Peter did say they were beasts who continually sinned and couldn't stop, cursed children made to be taken and destroyed. Notice also that Peter says that the condemnation of Sodom (a city completely filled with all manner of perverts and cruelty) was made an example to all those who after should so dwell. But perhaps presenting only these few Scriptures is not enough to convince many people. Here is another one from the Holy Ghost in Jude, another holy child of God,

> 6 And the angels which kept not their first estate, but left their own habitation, he hath reserved in everlasting chains under darkness unto the judgment of the great day.
> 7 Even as Sodom and Gomorrah, and the cities about them in like manner, giving themselves over to fornication, and going after strange flesh, are set forth an example, suffering the vengeance of eternal fire...
> 10 But these speak evil of those things which they know not: but what they know naturally, as brute beasts, in those things they corrupt themselves...
> 17 But beloved, remember ye the words which were spoken before of the apostles of our Lord Jesus Christ;
> 18 How that they told you there should be mockers in the last time, who should walk after their own ungodly lusts.
> 19 These be they who separate themselves, sensual, having not the Spirit.
> (Jude chapter 1)

There are considerable other Scriptures which I could also record from the New Testament but I feel that now having heard from Paul, Peter, and Jude on one accord concerning perversion, the only Scripture needful of being cited are the words of Jesus Christ Himself,

3 The Pharisees also came unto him, tempting him, and saying unto him, Is it lawful for a man to put away his wife for every cause?

4 And he answered and said unto them, Have ye not read, that he which made them at the beginning made them male and female,

5 And said, For this cause shall a man leave father and mother, and shall cleave unto his wife: and they twain shall be one flesh?

6 Wherefore they are no more twain, but one flesh. What therefore God hath joined together, let not man put asunder. (Matthew chapter 19)

The Lord Jesus is clearly saying that God set a precedent when He made the human being to be male and female and that any alteration of this is not acceptable. Actually, the *way* in which God created us is far deeper than many understand and I am speaking about our consciousness. In God's Creative Writing this is explained in depth along with *exactly* how and why the Trinity is what it is. Suffice it to say that man being created in the image of God parallels the depth of the Trinity and any alteration of this creates some of the deepest blasphemy, not just defying Earthly nature, but defying the very Essence of Reality itself! And *that* is why such changes into perversion create the Beast that was, and is not, and yet is! That description from Revelation chapter 17 verse eight is what you create with perversion!

Even though man was originally made alone by himself, he is not even permitted to return to being alone because God set a precedent when He said, It is not good for man to be alone, I will make him an help-meet for him. . . and the rib which He took from the man, made He a woman, and brought her unto the man. The woman, whom was made from the man, is a part of man and it is unlawful for one to hinder this union because in so doing they are destroying themselves, being made a part of one another to be one together. She is the part of the man that he no longer has within himself and he is the part of the woman which she no longer has around herself.

Yet, God magnified their oneness by giving them a free will to be one together in love, as well as one flesh. This free will unity is greater than the passive oneness they had before Eve was created because it is a free active oneness! And, yet, even in this freedom, they are a part of each other as demonstrated within all the children who come into the world being created half from the father and half from the mother.

It is bad enough when a man and woman separate or divorce from one another, but when a man or woman destroy any possibility or potential for them to be joined together in goodness, as perverts do, then they have blasphemed against the Holy Ghost in that that they have destroyed God's receptacle which was fashioned by God in a particular way to contain particular portions of His Spirit.

Self-destruction is not forgivable. Understand more deeply what I mean by, It is unlawful to *destroy this union*. It is unlawful before Almighty God to destroy the original making of the human being so that the man and woman no longer accept each as a part of one another. *That* is where the desire for unity in both flesh and spirit comes from, that each recognizes that together they are part of a whole! Understand that when God divided the woman from the man, this structure was passed down to *all* men and women who come after Adam and Eve as demonstrated by *exactly* what the children are made from- half the genes from the man and half from the woman. And their reproductive organs each reproduce exactly *half* of their genes to contribute to the next generation. Each half waits for the half that completes it.

Even eunuchs still recognize that the male and female are part of one another, though they are unable to join their flesh. Furthermore, Paul describes Jesus Christ as follows, By whom also God made the worlds, Christ being the brightness of His glory, and the express image of His person. . . Paul describes the woman as follows, The woman is the glory of the man. So, as Christ is the glory of the Father, even so is the woman the glory of the man! The woman manifests the goodness of God by embracing and upholding with all her heart, soul, mind and strength, the goodness he placed in the man even as Christ embraces and loves the Father with all His *Being*. The man manifests the goodness of God by fully loving and appreciating the woman as the glory of the goodness God made the man to be. He is not that glory, *she* is. All of this describes *complementary unity*, a perfect, balanced whole. *That* is the true image of God between the Father and the Son!

Adam named his wife Eve, because she was the mother of all living. As God created all through His Son (By whom also God made the worlds) even so God made the woman to bring forth man's children. When God said, Let us make man in our image, after our likeness. . . so God created man in His own image, in the image of God created He him, male and female created He them and blessed them, and called their name Adam in the day when they were created, well, this is the image of the Oneness of God, God the Father, and God the Son, being one God together and speaking, Let us make man in *our* image and likeness.

God never changes and, therefore, God's image is unchanging. Therefore, to attempt to change or destroy God's image is unforgivable because God will not be mocked. The reason why the man and the woman together were made in the image of God is because as the whole of God lives, so are we as a whole able to live in such perfection. But *anything* constructed differently from this is doomed to die, to fail, to be perverse in that the corrupted parts, since they have no unity, can only abuse, and destroy each other.

Therefore, Almighty God will not, cannot accept, receive, allow into His Kingdom, *any* perversity at all. Because there is no suitable vessel into which to pour his Spirit, their foundation having been self-destroyed away from being in the living image of God. *All* perversion is that kind of self-destruction and *that* is why it incurs such a wrath from God. It is also very dangerous to even support such abomination even *if* you are not like that yourself. That is why Jesus said, What therefore God has joined together, let not man put asunder. God knows best. Let me now continue with Christ's discourse. It *may* be that there is a solution here for the perverse,

> 7 They say unto him, Why did Moses then command to give a writing of divorcement, and to put her away?
> 8 He saith unto them, Moses because of the hardness of your hearts suffered you to put away your wives: but from the beginning it was not so.
> 9 And I say unto you, Whosoever shall put away his wife, except it be for fornication, and shall marry another, committeth adultery: and whoso marrieth her which is put away doth commit adultery.
> 10 His disciples say unto him, If the case of the man be so with his wife, it is not good to marry.
> 11 But he said unto them, All men cannot receive this saying, save they to whom it is given.

12 For there are some eunuchs, which were so born from their mother's womb: and there are some eunuchs, which were made eunuchs of men: and there be eunuchs, which have made themselves eunuchs for the kingdom of heaven's sake. He that is able to receive it, let him receive it. (Matthew chapter 19)

Jesus seems to allow for the dissimilation of God's making man and woman together concerning the case of fornication. Not really. Consider Christ's answer to his disciples when they said that if a man discovers his betrothed is not a virgin then it is better not to marry her. Jesus answered them that not all men in such a situation can put away their intended wives. Then Jesus made it very clear who was allowed to divorce their wives: eunuchs!

Eunuchs are men that no longer have testicles. They do not have the ability to produce the seed of life, nor the ability to even desire to mate. Therefore, since that man is not able to supply his wife with that duty of marriage with which she had already presumptuously acquainted herself, he may let her go. Otherwise, she would play the whore on her husband and be also guilty of further adultery, seeing that he could not satisfy her God-given desire. In such a situation, God allows the man to put away his wife since he cannot fulfil his duty to her. She is then free to return to the man with whom she had mated, since she never actually married her betrothed.

Originally, according to the Law of God, such should be stoned to death. However, as Jesus said, He that hath no sin, cast the first stone, and since God no longer desires to set an holy kingdom upon *this* earth, but in the new Earth to come, God suffers such people to exist in hopes that they will repent, even as Mary Magdalene repented. Now that the Holy Ghost is able to keep a person from sinning, it is not necessary for the holy children of God to rely on keeping sinners away from them, away from their promised land for them to stay holy. However, before the Holy Ghost, man was able to be beguiled through many women and for the sake of God's people, God did not suffer whores to lawfully exist.

Now, the real holy children of God can be right in the middle of intense sinners and it won't bother them because the Holy Ghost allows them to see through the Spirit and not only through the flesh, the flesh being made dead to sin by the Holy Ghost. Therefore, the children of God do not depend on the enforcement of rigid ordinances against sin and sinners, but they depend on the Holy Ghost to keep them pure.

I point out that a eunuch doesn't have to put away his betrothed if she desires to dwell with him. There are those holy children of God who live with their wives having never known them in the flesh, yet, rejoicing always together in the Holy Spirit of Jesus Christ and cleaving to one another by that Spirit. The image of God is preserved. I should also mention that many men and women join themselves together, or, they are joined together by some other man, but not by God. Jesus said, What therefore *God* hath joined together, let not man put asunder. Even so, man is supposed to do his best for the woman with whom he lays down. If they are not meant to be together by God then God will make this known. All one has to do is just ask.

My readers may be wondering where all this leads to a possible solution for the perverse. Let me quote another Holy Scripture from Jesus Christ that perhaps might offer a solution for the perverse. Remember, these are Jesus Christ's words, not mine,

> 29 And if thy right eye offend thee, pluck it out, and cast it from thee: for it is profitable for thee that one of thy members

should perish, and not that thy whole body should be cast into hell.

30 And if thy right hand offend thee, cut it off, and cast it from thee: for it is profitable for thee that one of thy members should perish, and not that thy whole body should be cast into hell. (Matthew chapter 5)

I would first like to point out that since the only men that are allowed to put away their wives are those that don't have the testicles to mate with her, then it follows that if a man does have his stones, then he is not allowed to put her away. Perverts do have the desire to mate (albeit, a confused mind and heart) and they do have testicles or ovaries. So what are they to do? Some may say that since they're not interested in the complementary sex to start with then none of this applies to them. However, Jesus made it perfectly clear that God set the precedent saying that since God made them male and female from the beginning, they are required to leave father and mother and cleave to each other. Therefore, no matter how confused the pervert might get, if they reject their duty to the other part of the whole human being, meaning man for woman and woman for man, then they have in effect put them away. Therefore there is only one escape for the pervert, since the complementary sex isn't good enough for them to make a life with.

Get neutered or spayed.

If the pervert becomes a eunuch then he is freed from his God given responsibility to the woman. As Jesus pointed out, there are those who for the kingdom of God's sake have indeed made themselves eunuchs. I ask the perverts to consider what a great sacrifice this would be to give glory unto God. Not everyone is able, nor has the opportunity to make such a sacrifice to glorify their love for God and Jesus Christ. If this sounds hard, just consider how much the holy children of God suffer for Christ's name sake.

Now, if some pervert happens to read all this and instead of being very humble, they might get angry, might even curse God, hmmm, might even think they are wise and *change* God, rewrite the Holy Scripture, redefine a bunch of things so they feel better, well, that's OK too! Because this is a different season. In *this* season God is sending you the solution to *all* your Earthly troubles. A bit is described in Daniel, and a bit in Revelation. God didn't want to tell ya too much. It's something *like* this from Revelation. You should search for it. These two have power to shut the heavens that it rain not in the days of their prophecy, and power to turn waters into blood and to smite the Earth with all manner of plagues as often as they will.

Now, let's just take a peek at what the holy children of God have had to put up with over the years. Some are tortured, beaten, ridiculed for sure, burnt up, flayed alive, crushed, pulled apart, oh well, use your imagination. Oh, even crucified. We've been the world's whipping post for a *very* long time. So, if castration sounds hard to the pervert, to the Beast's minions, well, we all have our crosses to bear and ourselves to deny, don't we?

Jesus said that in order to be saved, one must deny himself, pick up his cross, and follow Him. But think how much easier it really is for the pervert to deny himself than for normal men. After all, since the pervert's testicles or ovaries give them the drive to commit such wretched abominations, it should be a great joy to them to get rid of those troublesome organs. That is a lot easier for them to do than for a normal man because a normal man's testicles don't necessarily drive him to commit the really wretched sins, although they can mess him up some. The normal man will think, Well, I don't have to chop them off, after all, I'm not really sinning that badly. Yet even the least sin can keep that normal man out of the kingdom of God.

And there we have it. The perverts have a great opportunity and excuse to make themselves into eunuchs and escape a drive that sends so many of them to hell. Does this really sound hard? The anger and pain that perverts would feel if they read this only testifies that they have *no* feeling at all for God or Jesus Christ, since they are not ashamed of what they do and defend the utter abomination that they are.

One thing more. In Deuteronomy it says, Thou shall not suffer a Sodomite to be of the children of Israel. This means that not only is the perverse act forbidden and condemned, but the actual human beast, too. So, the only hope a pervert has is that *before* they ever become a full blown pervert, before they commit their first perverse act, when they first realize they are confused by being attracted to something that God forbids, well, rush and have yourself fixed just like folks do for their pets to calm them down and make them more agreeable. It *may* be that then God will accept them.

One more thing. When Jesus went about doing many miracles in many cities, there were those cities where only a few believed. He replied, and said, Woe unto you, for if the mighty works done in you would have been done in Sodom, she would be standing today, therefore, it shall be more tolerable for the city of Sodom than for you in the day of judgment! Why? God destroyed Sodom and Gomorrah because they had committed unforgivable sins and were unable to be saved. Yet, those cities that would not hear and believe Jesus Christ had a chance to be saved. They could have been saved but the religious (who made up a sizable population) just didn't want

PERVERTS (SODOMITES) JESUS SAID...

to be saved. Therefore, their punishment is greater because their wickedness becomes greater by rejecting the salvation and mercy that was possible for them to have.

There is another question that might pop into a perverts mind or others who want to fault God and not themselves. Well, if Sodom would have been spared by those miracles that Jesus did when he was here, why didn't God just do something like that anyway? Well, it just wasn't time for Jesus to come then. Also, Justice precluded the Lord doing *anything* more for them than what was done. And what *was* done was that Lot lived there for a long time and pleaded and tried to teach them better, not to mention that they *saw* the righteousness that he lived. He had even betrothed his daughters to them. None of it was heeded. And when they went to break down the door to brutalize the strangers and Lot and his daughters, that sealed their fate. Just because God knew that such miracles would have changed their minds, doesn't mean it was even right that they should be graced by them! Jesus performed all those wonders when He was here because the religious people then were a *lot* like they are now, halfway up Jacob's ladder but not at the top where they're supposed to be. Because of their *partial* love for God, Jesus gifted to them to behold *many* mercies and signs and wonders and even gave them seventy years after they helped put him to death. And then the Romans came and destroyed everything and many were slaughtered and worse.

So, to finish this chapter, I would like to record two more Scriptures from the Lord Jesus Christ,

> 14 And whosoever shall not receive you, nor hear your words, when ye depart out of that house or city, shake off the dust of your feet.

15 Verily I say unto you, It shall be more tolerable for the land of Sodom and Gomorrah in the day of judgment, than for that city. (Matthew chapter 10)

I say to the Christians and the religious, Please don't harden your hearts. Only holiness shall see God and the rest shall be lost. Think about this book. It is *obvious* I am not trying to win a popularity contest, not trying to sell a lot of books because honestly, what would be my market? Who would want to read about and truly subject themselves to the difficulties of true salvation? But, this is the whole truth. *Please* regard this warning from Jesus that He actually gave *before* we knew Him as Jesus,

20 Wisdom crieth without; she uttereth her voice in the streets:
21 She crieth in the chief place of concourse, in the openings of the gates: in the city she uttereth her words, saying,
22 How long, ye simple ones, will ye love simplicity? And the scorners delight in their scorning, and fools hate knowledge?
23 Turn you at my reproof: behold, I will pour out my spirit unto you, I will make known my words unto you.
24 Because I have called, and ye refused; I have stretched out my hand, and no man regarded;
25 But ye have set at naught all my counsel, and would none of my reproof:
26 I also will laugh at your calamity; I will mock when your fear cometh;
27 When your fear cometh as desolation, and your destruction cometh as a whirlwind; when distress and anguish cometh upon you.

28 Then shall they call upon me, but I will not answer; they shall seek me early, but they shall not find me:
29 For that they hated knowledge, and did not choose the fear of the Lord:
30 They would none of my counsel: they despised all my reproof.
31 Therefore shall they eat of the fruit of their own way, and be filled with their own devices.
32 For the turning away of the simple shall slay them, and the prosperity of fools shall destroy them.
33 But whoso hearkeneth unto me shall dwell safely, and shall be quiet from fear of evil.

CONCLUSION

I have reached the conclusion of this book and so it's fitting that I say a little about the conclusion of this world. It is written that at the time of the end when the transgressors are come to the full, a beast shall rise up out of the sea of peoples in the world. He shall magnify himself to the world above God and above every god that has heretofore been known. Through flattery and deceit, the anti-Christ becomes strong with a small people that is gathered out of this sea and through great wrath shall he destroy all goodness upon the face of the Earth by destroying God's holy people, and *everything* that has meaning of goodness! For God has suffered to give it all into the Beast's hand. Please remember the words of Jesus, Whosoever shall save his life shall lose it, but whosoever shall lose his life in this world for my namesake, shall save it. This is so the true children of God with true faith can rise again unto a better kingdom.

The Beast shall condemn many, *many* souls through his illusion of peace for he shall control the commerce of the Earth and feed and care for all those which receive his mark unto loyalty to him. The people of the world shall not consider that God has all power and He feeds them. They will believe this false god feeds and cares for them.

Yet, those filled with the Holy Ghost will be preserved and some of them will be standing when Jesus Christ appears.

Jesus mentions that at the time of the end it shall be as the days of Noah and the days of Sodom. I have heard many Christian leaders say that Jesus never said anything about perversion but that statement about Sodomites during the end of the world is more than sufficient, besides all the Scriptures I quoted in this book, but even the many I didn't quote.

Oh, you know how the Christian leaders *love* to read the Bible and so many so called great religious men's books, and how they love to quote them to teach you better? These Christians are so learned. Hmm, did any of them mention to you that the ani-Christ rises from a small people? That he shall not regard the desire of women? Funny, I *never* heard them mention that. Some of them mention the small people and wonder what that means but *none* mention the other Scripture. Well, look at that, it's right near to some Scriptures they love to quote. Ones like the anti-Christ will change God's laws and generally make everything backwards but they always seem to leave *that one* out, the one that tells you how really perverted the anti-Christ is. I wonder why they left out an important identity marker that distinguishes the anti-Christ.

Just before Jesus Christ reappears, the world will have been in the same condition as when God flooded the Earth and burnt up Sodom and Gomorrah. When Christ reappears then shall the people cry out to the mountains and to the rocks to hide them from an angry God but the rocks will answer back, and say, No hiding place here.

God shall destroy this world again, but this time by fire, not water. The transgressors coming to the full also indicates that the world is wholly given over to the sins of Sodom, and Jesus indicates that the same

~ CONCLUSION ~

condemnation shall come upon the world. I wish that people would seek God with all their hearts and search the Scriptures themselves, instead of relying on others to lead them blind and lull them to sleep.

In that day when Jesus will appear, the morning is going to be brighter than any morning ever seen, so bright a morning it shall be. The sun is going to rise in the East, as it always has, but the moon will seem as if it rises in the West. However, because so many other signs and wonders will have been done, the people of the world will not even notice until one hour before noonday. Then they shall fall out of the buildings to watch the last hour of the world. When the sun and moon meet together in the noonday sky, there shall be a great darkness such as never was before, so that one's hand will not be able to be seen right in front of their face. The moon will drip in blood back to the Earth, and then, where the sun and moon had been, shall the form of a great Light begin to appear, growing larger and larger, and Jesus will be that Light returning on the same cloud that He left upon.

But, He *doesn't* come here. Jesus stops in the midair and the holy children of God will rise up to meet Him. The rest of the ungodly will be left down here in pitch darkness until judgment day. So I say to the people of the world, if anyone claims to be Jesus Christ here on Earth, don't believe him because Jesus Christ is not setting foot on this Earth anymore. When Jesus comes, all the holy angels will be with him! So, to conclude this book, I record the following Scripture as Jesus Christ spoke it. May God the Father, God the Son, and God the Holy Ghost bless you all. Amen.

20 And when he was demanded of the Pharisees, when the kingdom of God should come, he answered them and said, The kingdom of God cometh not with observation:

21 Neither shall they say, Lo here! Or, Lo there! For, behold, the kingdom of God is within you.

22 And he said unto the disciples, The days will come, when ye shall desire to see one of the days of the Son of man, and ye shall not see it.

23 And they shall say unto you, See here; or, see there: go not after them, nor follow them.

24 For as the lightening, that lighteth out of the one part under heaven, shineth unto the other part under heaven; so shall the Son of man be in his day.

25 But first must he suffer many things, and be rejected of this generation.

26 And as it was in the days of Noah, so shall it be also in the days of the Son of man.

27 They did eat, they drank, they married wives, they were given in marriage, until the day that Noah entered into the ark, and the flood came, and destroyed them all.

28 Likewise also as it was in the days of Lot; they did eat, they drank, they bought, they sold, they planted, they builded;

29 But the same day that Lot went out of Sodom it rained fire and brimstone from heaven, and destroyed them all.

30 Even thus shall it be in the day when the Son of man is revealed.

31 In that day, he which shall be upon the housetop, and his stuff in the house, let him not come down to take it away: and he that is in the field, let him likewise not return back.

32 Remember Lot's wife.

33 Whosoever shall seek to save his life shall loose it; and whosoever shall lose his life shall preserve it. (Luke chapter 17)

www.ingramcontent.com/pod-product-compliance
Lightning Source LLC
Chambersburg PA
CBHW072157070526
44585CB00015B/1178